Castles,
Follies &
Four-Leaf
Clovers

Castles, Follies & Four-Leaf Clovers

ADVENTURES ALONG IRELAND'S ST DECLAN'S WAY

ROSAMUND BURTON

ALLEN&UNWIN

First published in 2011

Copyright © Rosamund Burton 2011

Allen & Unwin
Sydney, Melbourne, Auckland, London

83 Alexander Street
Crows Nest NSW 2065
Australia
Phone: (61 2) 8425 0100
Fax: (61 2) 9906 2218
Email: info@allenandunwin.com
Web: www.allenandunwin.com

Cataloguing-in-Publication details are available
from the National Library of Australia
www.trove.nla.gov.au

ISBN 978 1 74175 952 5

Map by Squirt Creative
Set in 11/14.5 pt Adobe Garamond Pro by Bookhouse, Sydney
Printed and bound in Australia by the SOS Print + Media Group

10 9 8 7 6 5 4 3

For Paul and Arabella Burton

Contents

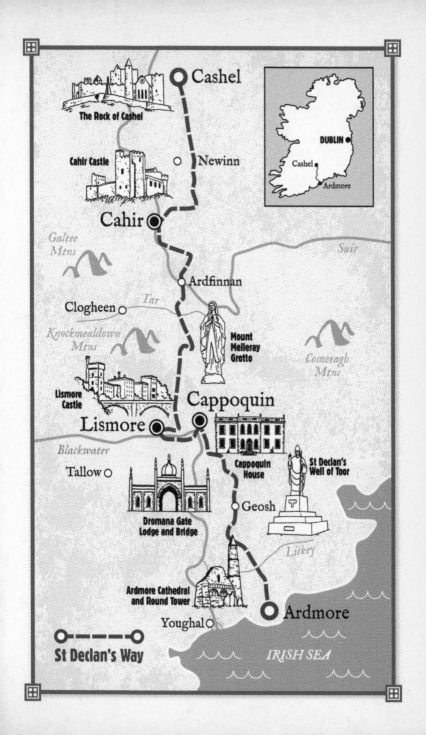

Cashel

The Rock of Cashel

Cahir Castle

- Newinn

Cahir

Galtee Mtns

Suir

- Ardfinnan

Tar

- Clogheen

Knockmealdown Mtns

Mount Melleray Grotto

Comeragh Mtns

Lismore Castle

Cappoquin

Lismore

Blackwater

- Tallow

Cappoquin House

St Declan's Well of Toor

Dromana Gate Lodge and Bridge

- Geosh

Lickey

Ardmore Cathedral and Round Tower

- Youghal

Ardmore

IRISH SEA

St Declan's Way

DUBLIN

Cashel

Ardmore

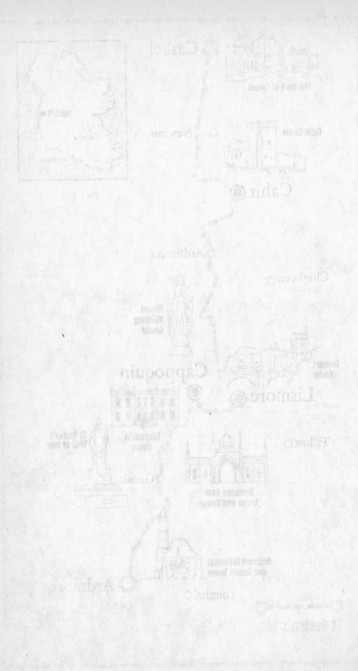

Introduction

Peeple are quick to tell me I'm not Irish, but if you were to put a label on me it could say, 'Made in Ireland'. I was born here and Ireland has shaped me for over half my life.

Part of the reason for walking along the little known St Declan's Way from the Rock of Cashel in County Tipperary to the fishing village of Ardmore in County Waterford was to rediscover the Irish part of me.

Although it's named after the saint who converted so many people in the region to Christianity, this ancient route is neither Christian nor pagan, but transcends both of these. Along the way I found sacred wells and holy springs, walked up narrow mountain paths, down main streets of towns and villages, and hacked my way along overgrown tracks beside rivers.

I also discovered that other worlds coexist with ours— worlds of miracles and mysticism. I visited the statue of the Virgin Mary at Mount Melleray grotto which in 1985 over a period of ten days was seen moving and heard talking. I learnt about the miraculous bin at the Cistercian monastery that never emptied and provided grain for both the monks and the poor for months during a time of famine. I saw a photograph of the little fairy hat found at Castle Doddard on the Knockmealdown Mountains.

In Ireland people are civilised like nowhere else in the world. In an era when social interaction is increasingly no longer given time, here people naturally start a conversation whenever there is an opportunity. Like the man I was sitting next to in a restaurant who told me about the donkey that smoked cigarettes and a pipe.

It's easy to lose our connection with ourselves, others and also our environment. Caught up in an increasingly frenetic world of money-making and career-building our minds are forever focusing on the future, and fearful of what it might bring, that the present moment is often lost.

Walking everyday I was continually brought back to the joy and glory of what was happening here and now. The sheer delight in the national game of hurling, when the Waterford team made the All-Ireland final for the first time in 45 years. The Irish love of horses, seen during a day at the Tallow Horse Fair. The heartfelt recognition of the divine present in every moment by a small convent of Cistercian nuns.

I was made aware of the interconnectedness of life. I could see the impact that the demise of the local chicken business was likely to have on the whole community. Here history is part of everyday life. People often refer back a hundred fifty years, frequently four hundred, and it's as if St Patrick, St

Brigid and St Declan are living still. In this small area of rural Ireland people's lives are intricately interwoven with each other and have been for generations, often in ways that are totally unexpected. It was Sir Walter Raleigh, who once owned Lismore Castle, that planted the first potato in Ireland, little knowing the part the tuber would play years later in the country's cruel fate.

I visited many of the Norman castles along the way, which are now either inhabited by colourful, eccentric Anglo-Irish, or are ivy-covered ruins in the gardens of their large Georgian houses. In the pouring rain I stood in front of the exquisite and totally incongruous Hindu style Gothic gate lodge and bridge of Dromana, where the gatekeeper turned away King Edward VII.

This is also a journey of belonging. What it means to belong on many levels. As humans we yearn to belong and yet we also long for freedom. We are forever trying to balance the two. I found what started as a walk became a pilgrimage, which gave me not only a greater understanding of what it means to belong in a community, but also, to my complete surprise, to the church, which I thought I'd left behind me many years ago when I turned to meditation and Eastern philosophies.

I don't usually get lost, but I always lose my way in Ireland. I think it's synonymous with the country, as even the tourist board promotes it as part of the Irish experience. Walking St Declan's Way, despite the map, I got lost many times. Also, because my journey was not only a physical one, but emotional and spiritual, it was fraught with twists and turns and blind alleys, and in many ways was like that loved Celtic symbol, the labyrinth. And the times I felt most lost were often when I was closest to my destination.

If you would like to walk St Declan's Way after reading this book please don't be put off by where I went left when I should have gone right, or turned back when I might have gone on. With each person's footsteps the way becomes clearer, but also the gift of getting lost is you never know what you might find.

1

The map

Many years ago an Irish friend lent me a map of an ancient highway which threads its way along quiet country lanes, grassy tracks and riverside paths, passing a string of castles and fairy forts, small villages and miraculous wells. Stretching 60 miles between the fishing village of Ardmore on Ireland's south coast and the town of Cashel in County Tipperary, this age-old pilgrim route was made famous by Ireland's beloved Saint Declan, who pre-dates Saint Patrick. I instantly wanted to walk St Declan's Way, but it wasn't the right time. So I photocopied the map and filed it away.

When I've all but forgotten my dream I have a small window of opportunity to return to Ireland and follow this historic way. Excited at the possibility of this adventure I take the photocopy out of the drawer where I'd stashed it years earlier. My heart sinks to see the black and white copy has faded over time. I realise I could never find my way using this sad piece of paper.

What's worse is that the friend who lent me the map originally has now died, so I have no idea how I can get hold of a copy. For a moment I fear this is just a pipedream. But I decide to ring the local Irish tourist office to see if someone there can help me.

'I've heard the path is very overgrown,' is all Norma, who answers the telephone, can tell me. She would love to walk St Declan's Way, she adds, but can't help me find a map.

As I stare at the photocopy on the table in front of me I can't think who else to ring or what to do next. Then I notice in the bottom corner the name of the company that produced the map and a telephone number. I dial it, and a man called Barry answers.

Barry tells me he did the walk ten years ago, but from what he's heard the way marks are now faded and the path has not been maintained. He remembers the map, but it's out of print. However, he gives me the number of Richard Lincoln in Ardmore who, he says, might be able to help me.

Delighted to have this lead I make the call and ask to speak to Richard Lincoln.

'He went to Africa yesterday,' the woman at the other end replies promptly. His departure sounds very finite. There is a long silence on the line. Before I hang up, in a final punt I explain that I want to walk St Declan's Way and am looking for a map. It transpires that Richard is a gas engineer working in Africa for a few weeks and I am talking to his wife Mary. She tells me that Richard's mother, an historian, spent 30 years retracing St Declan's Way. Mary owns Ardmore Pottery and suggests I drop in and pick up a map. I can hardly believe my luck. Especially when I explain I am on the other side of the globe and she offers to post a map to me.

As I ponder on her spontaneous generosity, I realise how often in Ireland people go out of their way to help others. It's one of the many traits that I cherish about this country.

Despite the fact I live half a world away, part of me will always belong to Ireland. Perhaps it is the pain of unrequited love, the way this country has of welcoming me with open arms and yet at the same time always holding me at arm's length, constantly creating within me the sense that, although it is where I was born, I do not really have a place here.

Ireland is like a lover who always gives me the most magical time, but does not believe in marriage and living happily ever after. So, despite returning again and again, mesmerised by its beauty and its people, its myths and its history, and always feeling that there is nowhere more wonderful than this, I am always thrust back out into the world.

Nothing is forgotten here. The past is always present. The numerous ruins, slowly decaying in the wind and the rain and dotted across the country's green face like small scars, stand as constant reminders of what has occurred over the centuries.

I love the vibrant greenness and rugged landscape of Ireland. I love its numerous freshwater springs presided over by the Virgin Mary or heralded for their healing properties. And the acknowledgement of ghosts and fairies and other mysterious phenomena in Ireland I think has given me a recognition of the mystical, and an understanding that not everything that occurs in life can be explained.

I adore the Irish humour and the phenomenal natural wit and ability to make conversation. I laugh in Ireland in a way I do nowhere else. People feel it is their duty to entertain you and amuse you, and also they naturally want to talk to you. I love the acceptance of people's eccentricity and idiosyncrasies here.

Whenever I'm back in Ireland I am amazed by people's intelligence and acumen, and the refusal of the Irish to conform and kow-tow. After growing up in England with its hierarchical class system, I think Ireland has given me a true understanding of equality. Whatever someone's background or social standing there is an innate self-esteem inherent in its people and despite its turbulent history, an absolute refusal to be subservient to someone just because they are in a position of power.

That said I am driven mad by the pettiness and the divisiveness caused by religion. Like many I struggle to accept the pain and misery that people find themselves in because they think they should do the 'right' thing. The loveless marriages. The young lives lost looking after manipulative parents. And then there are the intelligent, talented people who turn to drink and end up blubbering alcoholics. Sometimes I want to weep and shake people out of their pathetic complacency and force them to change.

With the period of rapid economic growth from the mid 1990s for just over a decade, known as the Celtic Tiger, Ireland became a far more vibrant place, but also a victim of its own progress. More families with two cars meant more traffic and new motorways and fewer old men in tweed jackets riding black bicycles along narrow country roads.

Ireland has changed considerably in the last 25 years, and a certain wildness has been lost. No longer are small boys riding through the streets of Dublin on the back of lorries. There are fewer street hawkers although the women with their stalls at Moore Street are still singing out the prices of their fruit and vegetables, and no doubt the candid woman on the fish stall rebuking a customer fingering the cod: 'Them's fish, not pricks. They don't improve with the handling.'

Some say people cast off tradition and savoured the taste of materialism. One woman summed it up. Talking about a local whitegoods shop, she said, 'You'd see things in there you never saw before and it would fill you with wanting.' Now the Celtic Tiger has been shot in the foot and the global financial downturn has hit Ireland particularly hard. Once again the Irish are emigrating in their thousands to find work and opportunities overseas, while so many of those who remain struggle to make ends meet.

But my journey is not just through Ireland today, but a trip back in time to a world of saints, fairies, ghosts and other mysteries, and deep into the heart of Ireland's spirituality and sacredness.

When I tell Irish friends I am walking St Declan's Way I get a flurry of emails warning me about the perpetual rain and graphic descriptions of flooded towns. I know the Irish often wile away beautiful sunny days with stories of the terrible weather, but I actually like the Irish rain, particularly if it's soft. The droplets are so fine it's like being sprayed with a light mist, which permeates every pore of your skin. Whenever I'm out in that soft rain I feel as if I'm having an expensive beauty treatment. Perhaps that is why during the wettest Irish summer for 150 years I have decided to undertake this walk.

I tell my husband, Stephen, that from all accounts St Declan's Way is in parts very overgrown, and it might mean a fair amount of hacking through brambles and nettles.

'Thank God St Patrick banished all the snakes,' he remarks. Then, despite the promise along the way of plenty of pubs serving pints of cool dark velvety Guinness, announces that he won't be joining me.

2

Coming home to the castle

When the map arrives in the post suddenly my trip seems real. In the midst of planning the walk and where to stay, buying and borrowing clothing, and other preparations, I find myself thinking about my years in Ireland.

I was born in County Down in Northern Ireland. My father was land agent at Mount Stewart at the time. But when I was only six months old we moved to Herefordshire, and I grew up in England.

In 1980, soon after I left school, my father got a job as a land agent looking after the Duke of Devonshire's Irish estates in Lismore, midway between Ardmore and Cashel along St Declan's Way. Our new home was the east wing of Lismore Castle.

We set off for Ireland the day after my eighteenth birthday party. I piled into the back of my parents' car with my cousins, Sophie and Carolyn, and we headed for Pembroke in South Wales where we were catching the all-night ferry to Ireland.

It was the first of many rough trips across the Irish Sea over the next few years. People were throwing up before the boat had even left the dock. Sophie and I lay head to toe in a narrow bunk, with Carolyn in the top bunk of the two-berth cabin. I woke up in the middle of the night to hear the sounds of lorries crashing against their chains on one of the lower decks. The ferry came into Cork Harbour in the early morning, and it was an overcast December day as we drove out of Cork along the River Lee towards Lismore.

I had seen a postcard of Lismore Castle with its numerous towers and turrets rising up from the bank of the Blackwater River, so I knew what it looked like. But seeing it for the first time I was awestruck by its magnificence. It seemed surreal that we were living in such a spectacular place and to be actually driving under the arch of the seventeenth-century riding house. As we came through the high stone archway of the gatehouse tower and into the enormous courtyard, I felt I was in a dream.

Straight ahead was the impressive entrance to the main part of the castle where the duke and duchess stayed. The duchess, known as Debo, was the youngest of the six famous Mitford girls. To the right of the imposing front entrance was the east wing and a tall circular castellated tower with an arched blue wooden door at its base. This was our front door. The first floor of the east wing had been done up for my parents. My mother, Marabella, used to call it the train because it was a very long corridor with rooms off it. I later discovered that the reason for this unconventional layout was that the duchess's sister, Lady Diana Mosley, was storing her furniture in some of the rooms below. Diana had married Sir Oswald Mosley, leader of the British Union of Fascists, and had Adolf Hitler as a guest of honour at the wedding.

Beyond the east wing adjoining the gatehouse tower was my father's office, with a large bay window overlooking the lower garden. It had a fireplace in the corner, where, except for hot summer days, a fire was usually lit, as he felt the cold. He would sit at his very large leather-topped wooden desk, squinting through his monocle at reports on the castle's dry rot. In the main office directly below sat Miss Casey with her small antiquarian black typewriter, which looked like something from a museum. Most offices had electric typewriters, but Miss Casey refused to use one. Her machine was so old when she typed some of the letters floated above the rest.

That first Christmas holiday my cousins and I explored room after room of the sprawling castle, which had been built by the English Prince John more than 800 years before. Later it was owned by Sir Walter Raleigh, that favourite of Queen Elizabeth I, who was renowned for bringing the potato and tobacco back from America.

Occasionally on our walks along the river and through the woodlands below the castle we would meet men in tweed jackets and caps whose accents were so thick we were unable to understand more than a few words. Despite their conversation being incomprehensible I was so thrilled that they wanted to talk to us. Having grown up among the far more reserved English I was amazed by everyone's friendliness. Even going shopping in the town was a social event. Florence and Ann

9

McCarthy who owned the Wine Vaults, and their children who took turns to work at the till, would always chat. The two Miss Willoughbys, who had the paper shop, would regale us every time we went in on the beauty of Lismore and the walks that we should do.

On the Sunday before Christmas we went to the carol service at the Lismore Cathedral. Frail Miss Nelly was on the organ. The small Church of Ireland congregation only filled the front third of the pews. Our feet and hands were numb with the cold of the huge stone building. We belted out the familiar Christmas tunes, and the sound of our voices floated up to the ornate ceiling high above us. Then on Christmas Eve we went to the little church at Fountain for midnight mass. The path from the gate to the church door was lined either side with candles. It was a cold frosty night, but inside the church was warm, and the pews full of people. I was so touched by the community spirit in that tiny church on Christmas Eve.

That first Christmas we were introduced to West Waterford's Anglo-Irish. The Anglo-Irish have a strong allegiance to both England and Ireland. Some of their families arrived in Ireland with the Normans 800 years ago. Others were given land for their loyalty to the English crown, while others again were Irish tribal leaders, who became Protestants out of political necessity. They are likely to join the Irish Guards and fight for king and country, and often send their children to school in England, yet would hate to be thought of as English. Their love of Ireland is deep and abiding.

Living in faded grandeur, with a love of hunting, fishing and shooting and with a great regard for etiquette, they are also often eccentric and delight in breaking all the rules. So although they might always change for dinner and sit down at a long mahogany table set with the family silver, they are just as likely to be found trading at a horse fair or dancing on a table in a pub. They rarely complain but carry on stoically as they did in the 1920s when the IRA burnt many of their houses to the ground. They are also known for their wry sense of humour, being fine observers of life around them and never so tedious as to take it too seriously.

Nearly every evening we would dress up and go to a drinks party, dinner party or a dance. On New Year's Day we went to an egg nog party given by an American couple over the mountain in Tipperary. I remember feeling distinctly unsure whether this warm frothy brandy-based drink full of egg and cream was easing my hangover or adding to it. After the party we went to collect a golden cocker spaniel puppy which my parents had bought. The drive back over the Knockmealdown Mountains was spent thinking of names for this little ball of fur. Egg Nog Dog was the name that stuck and for the next ten years the gardens of Lismore Castle would reverberate with one of us screeching her name.

A few days into the new year I went back to England with my cousins. As I had decided I wanted to be an actress, my mother had signed me up for a three-month secretarial course. 'So you have another way to earn a living apart from treading the boards', she said while softly singing Noel Coward's song *Don't Put Your Daughter on the Stage*.

11

My parents drove us to Waterford city. It was with great reluctance that I got the train from there to Rosslare and then the ferry across the Irish Sea. I had instantly fallen in love with my new home. But belonging there was a different story altogether.

3

On my way

Once in the West of Ireland I asked an old man for directions and his response was, 'I wouldn't start from here'. I don't think anyone would advise starting halfway round the world when planning to walk from Cashel to Ardmore, but that is where I happen to be. Now I live in Australia. I came to Sydney for work and instantly fell in love with this beautiful vibrant city and its sandy beaches and spectacular harbour. I started sailing, then met Stephen at Middle Harbour Yacht Club, fell in love with him, and a little over a year later we married.

It's strange arriving at Cork Airport and not being met by anyone. Even though I usually enjoy being alone, I instantly feel lonely and also sad at how our family life has changed. Normally, I would be going to Camphire Hill, the cottage 5 miles from Lismore, where my parents moved after Paul, my father, retired. But he died several years ago and the cottage was sold last year. Marabella, my mother, who now lives in the nearby coastal town of Dungarvan, is staying with my uncle in England for a few weeks. So I catch a bus from the airport to Cork's central bus station and from there another one to Cashel.

As the bus races out of Cork past the cargo ships tied up along the River Lee, I think about my first Easter at Lismore, when the Duke and Duchess of Devonshire were in residence. The morning after I arrived I was walking through the lower garden with the dogs. The azaleas and camellias were a blaze of whites, pinks and oranges. Egg Nog ran ahead and disappeared into a camellia bush. As I approached a man in a new raincoat and pair of black gumboots with a large machine gun under his arm appeared from behind it. A couple of years earlier Lord Mountbatten, the Queen's cousin, had been killed by an IRA bomb while staying at his family home in Sligo. As a result the Duke and Duchess were thought by the Irish government to require the protection of the Garda, the Irish police, while they were in the country.

Most days the Duke and his fishing buddies, accompanied by the plain-clothed Garda, would go fishing. The Duchess usually remained at the castle. We would occasionally meet her walking in the garden or along the road up to the dairy and the castle farm, always accompanied by her loyal black and white collie.

That Easter Sophie, Carolyn and I also met the poet Thomas McCarthy, a small man in his mid-20s with curly brown hair and sparkling eyes, who, much to our astonishment, did not drink. But lack of alcohol did not dampen his ability to talk. He explained with pride that in ancient

Ireland poets were second only to kings. He told us stories about the local history and said that Lismore was once known throughout Europe as a great centre of learning. The castle had previously been the site of a monastery, and the monks used to live hermit-style along the river in caves. Later that holiday when Carolyn and I walked through the woods above the river we found little rocky enclaves and imagined the monks 1300 years earlier living in these damp tiny spaces. Along the inches there was the salmon weir originally made by the monks. One day when Egg Nog took off into the woodlands after a rabbit, we followed a track up to a couple of lakes which later I discovered were known as the monks' pools.

I came back to Lismore a few months later. As my father found he was unable to persuade Miss Casey to use any machine other than her archaic typewriter with its flying letters, I was given the part-time job of typing all his documents and correspondence. Apart from the few weeks during the summer when the main part of the castle was rented to rich Americans, I was able to wander wherever I wanted. One afternoon I climbed up into the gatehouse tower and found boxes of accounts going back 200 years. Often I tiptoed through the derelict west wing, carefully avoiding the rotten floorboards.

That summer I first met Molly Keane. She was 76 years old and her novel, *Good Behaviour*, which was subsequently short-listed for the Booker Prize, was about to be published. She told me she was pretending to be 80 in the hope that people might think 'poor old lady' and be nice about her book. She had begun writing to supplement her dress allowance and published her first novel at the age of seventeen, under the pseudonym MJ Farrell, so her hunting and fishing friends would not discover she had a literary bent. She wrote ten novels and four plays which were all directed by John Gielgud. Then some scathing reviews and the death of her adored husband, Bobby, stopped her writing for twenty years. It was only when her friend, the actress Googie Withers, came to stay and was ill in bed for a couple of days that Molly took a manuscript out of a drawer for her to read. That manuscript was *Good Behaviour*.

Marabella and I often used to drive down to Ardmore and have tea with Molly in her house overlooking the sea. While we were there we would usually visit the ruined cathedral and the little stone building in which St Declan is believed to be buried, and also walk along the cliffs and to the holy well. It was here at Ardmore, where St Declan founded a monastery 1600 years ago, that I first became interested in his story.

Declan was a direct descendant of Tuathal Teachmhar of the Déisi tribe, who was the High King of Ireland and King of Tara 2000 years ago. Later the Déisi tribe were expelled from Tara and their land in County Meath. The Déisi tribe divided into three branches. St Declan's lot was given lands by the King of Munster in County Tipperary and County Waterford. These lands became known as the Déise pronounced day-sha, or the Decies, the anglised version of the name. The Déise of St Declan's time covered a similar region to the Roman Catholic Diocese of Waterford and Lismore today, stretching as far north into County Tipperary as Cahir.

However, nowadays it's the area of County Waterford that is known as the Déise.

Declan was born at Drumroe just south of Lismore. At the time of his birth seven men saw a ball of fire blazing above the house, and they prophesised that this baby would become a bishop.

The priest who baptised Declan also foretold his future greatness, predicting that his good deeds and sanctity would be known through Ireland, and that he would convert the Déisi from paganism to Christianity. He said that the baby must be brought up with good care and sent to study at the age of seven, so Declan was brought up by his uncle, and then educated by a devout man.

After he completed his studies, Declan travelled to Rome and was made a bishop by the Pope. On his way home through Italy he met St Patrick, who was subsequently also made a bishop. Apparently, they made a bond of mutual fraternity before going their separate ways, Patrick to Rome and Declan to Ireland.

The Life of St Declan, which is the source of what we know about St Declan today, is believed to have been written in about the eighth century, but it could have been centuries earlier or later. Also, the Celts never differentiated between myth and history, so very little is known for sure about him. But I want to find out what I can, and how he is remembered today.

I also want to learn more about this part of Ireland which so fascinates me, to understand its history, its people and its land. And perhaps to understand a little more of the country

I come from. For me Ireland has always felt like home, but I have also had the strong sense of being an outsider.

The more I think about belonging the less I understand what it means. I assume that people who have always stayed in one place must feel they belong there, and part of me wishes I was one of those people who just know they are part of a community. But mine has been a nomadic existence.

In his novels and plays the brilliant Irish writer, Sebastian Barry, focuses a great deal on belonging. Many of his main characters are people who do not fit in. 'We are always longing to be at home,' he once said in an interview, 'and I think it is a double distress to be told you are at home, so why don't you feel at home?'

4

Perfect potatoes

From what information I have managed to glean on St Declan's Way and looking at the map, it appears that it is usually walked from Ardmore to Cashel, but I want to end up in Ardmore, so I have decided to walk it the other way round. I speak to Thomas McCarthy on the telephone and asks if he thinks this is a problem.

'God will get you whether you are coming or going,' he replies.

So here I am heading for Cashel. It is late afternoon when I first catch sight of the Rock of Cashel, the distinctive collection of church buildings sitting high on the hill above the plains of Tipperary. The bus stops on the main street of the town near the Celtic cross memorial to Archbishop Croke. I go immediately into the city hall, next to the memorial, where there is an information centre and discover there is a hostel on the outskirts of town.

As I walk towards the hostel, the town, with its population of 2500 people, quickly gives way to fields. A herd of Friesian cows stare at me from behind a stone wall. Behind them large black crows, the foretellers of death, sit on top of the grass-covered arches of the ruined Hore Abbey, which was disbanded at the time of Henry VIII's dissolution of the monasteries. On the other side of the road the Rock of Cashel rises in its splendour. This was once the home of the King of Munster, before it later became a powerful religious centre. The remains of the thirteenth-century cathedral and the well-preserved tall thin round tower with its conical roof hover above the other ecclesiastical buildings.

The hostel is a converted farmhouse and immaculately clean. Tom O'Brien, the owner, gives me a quick tour. The main room is a combined kitchen, dining and sitting room. In front of the wood-burning stove a Frenchman and his son are sitting on the floor playing cards. A German woman comes in and starts preparing vegetables at the sink, while her child stands in the hall singing a nursery rhyme. I feel I am on the Continent rather than in Ireland. Tom opens a door into a room of bunk beds. I choose a top bunk near the window before making my way back into town to get something to eat.

Across the road from the hostel I find a stile over a stone wall and follow the path up the hill towards the Rock of Cashel. Swallows dive and circle above the long grass and white heads of ground elder. On either side of the path red clover is growing and clumps of ragwort and purple knapweed.

This side of the Rock of Cashel is rural. Behind me, beyond the hostel, are green fields. When I reach the top of the hill I can see the town below me, and above me is the Rock. It is quiet up here and there is no one else around. So

I sit, watching the daylight fade, with the round tower and the other buildings silhouetted against the evening sky, and starlings and jackdaws circling around them.

I remember all the times I travelled through Cashel when I was living in Dublin. There was a bus service from Dublin to Lismore on Friday evening, but during the week I used to get a lift from the fruit and vegetable market on the quays on the Dowds' truck, which travelled to Dublin three days a week for fresh produce. Usually Peter Dowd drove the truck, but at one stage the Dowd brothers employed a driver who was very fond of his CB radio. He'd spend most of the four-hour journey chatting on the radio. All the people on the CB radio had names which sounded like characters from a comic. One winter evening as we were heading to Lismore the driver had a very animated conversation on the radio with one Foxy Lady, and instead of following the main road he turned off and wound his way along a series of narrow country roads before pulling up outside a cottage. In he went to see Foxy Lady, leaving me sitting in the cab getting colder and crankier by the minute, but I couldn't complain as I was getting a free lift. Finally the driver emerged and we continued on to Lismore.

Prompted by hunger I walk past the ruined Dominican abbey, another victim of Henry VIII's reformation, and into Ladyswell Street.

I peer through the windows of several restaurants and pubs, but feel both selfconscious and indecisive so don't enter any of them. Eventually, I go into Daverns, a pub on the main street. The front room is full of families having dinner. As all the tables are full, one of the mature ladies behind the bar tells me to sit at the bar on the lounge side. Longing to dine alone unnoticed, or squeeze in beside a group of people I can talk to, I find myself sitting on a high stool, not near enough to anyone to start a conversation, but in clear view of everyone. I order a glass of Guinness and a plate of potatoes and try to interest myself in the *Rose of Tralee* on television.

I watch as a glass of Guinness is poured for me, longing to taste it but knowing that this is a slow process. Initially it is left to settle on the counter, before being topped up, so the creamy head is right at the top of the glass, and finally it is handed to me. I wait another minute or so for it to settle again. Only when it changes from a moving brown mass of liquid to a still black do I take my first sip. It is exquisite.

A pile of potatoes garnished with parsley is placed in front of me, and immediately my discomfort dissolves. Irish potatoes are unlike potatoes anywhere else in the world, and cooking them is an art form. To my delight these are cooked to perfection. They are soft and floury and melt in the mouth. As I slowly eat, savouring the flavour, I am struck by a glorious sense of freedom. I have three weeks ahead of me to do this walk. For the first time in my life I have no commitments and my time is my own. It feels great.

5

The Rock of Cashel

My journey begins at the Rock of Cashel, so after making myself some breakfast, I walk back up the path I followed yesterday, and pay the entrance fee to see the impressive ecclesiastical building on the top of this high limestone hill. Standing on top of the Rock I feel as if I am on top of the world. Below on one side are the town roofs and on the other lush green fields stretching for miles. I look down at the ruins of Hore Abbey where the enclosed order of Cistercian monks once lived their lives of prayer and contemplation and manual labour. Looking north I see in the distance the Devil's Bit. The gap is there, it is said, because the devil took a bite out of the mountain. In doing so he broke his teeth and dropped his mouthful, making the Rock of Cashel.

Cashel comes from the Irish word *caiseal* meaning fortress. Before it was handed over to the church 900 years ago, the Rock of Cashel was the home of the kings of Munster and rivalled Tara as the main centre of power in Ireland. In Irish the Rock of Cashel is called *Carraig Phádraig* which means the Rock of Patrick. Here St Patrick baptised Munster king Aongus MacNatfrich. I join a tour and Anne the guide tells us that St Patrick in his fervour was banging his crozier up and down not into the ground, as he thought, but onto King Aongus's foot. The king assumed this was part of the ceremony, so despite the pain, said nothing.

How Christianity first came to Ireland is unknown. A bishop called Palladius was sent there in 431, and Patrick arrived a year later. Ireland's patron saint, Patrick, is often given credit for converting the Irish to Christianity, but before his arrival St Declan was preaching and baptising people and building churches. St Declan travelled from Ardmore to Cashel, along the ancient highway I am about to walk, to convert King Aongus to Christianity. However, although King Aongus was happy for Declan to preach to his people, he refused to be baptised by him on the grounds that Declan was of the Déisi, the tribe whose land was to the southeast of Cashel, and Aongus was head of the Eoghanacht tribe, which had always been hostile to the Déisi. Later when King Aongus heard that Patrick had come to Ireland as a bishop and missionary, he left Cashel to go and meet him, and immediately professed his Christianity and was baptised.

When Patrick came to Ireland many of the kings and rulers came and paid homage to him. An angel came to Declan and told him to go to the place in south County Tipperary where Patrick was at the time. Declan took with him all the people of the Déise who he had converted to Christianity except the

king of the Déise and his household who said they would be
baptised but continually procrastinated.

Then Patrick returned to Cashel and Declan went with
him. There it was ordained by Patrick and King Aongus that
as the Irish should serve Patrick, so should the people of the
Déise serve Declan:

> Déaglán, Pádraig na nDéise,
> Na Déise ag Déaglán go bráth

Meaning 'Declan is the Patrick of the Déise, May the Déise
remain with Declan forever.'

Dotted between the buildings on the Rock are numerous
gravestones. A large Celtic cross on which is carved a motif
of Celtic knotwork marks the grave of someone called Ellen
Fitzgerald. It is said that St Patrick, or possibly St Declan,
combined the Christian cross with the pre-historic sun symbol,
a cross inside a circle, symbolising the joining together of
heaven and earth with the circle of creation. As I look at the
Celtic cross I realise how early Christianity used the pagan
symbols and beliefs to bring people to Christ. But I also
realise that within this Christian symbol are still the old
meanings—the circle representing eternity and the cross the
four directions.

It is also said that St Patrick used the shamrock to explain
the mystery of the Holy Trinity—the Father, the Son and the
Holy Ghost as three separate beings but part of one God.

Next to the shell of the vast thirteenth-century cathedral,
with its arches and high walls, is the round tower. Built 900
years ago it is still in perfect condition. The distinctive round

towers of Ireland, with walls that taper in to their conical caps, have remained a bit of a mystery. Thought to have first been built as bell towers, these edifices are unique to Ireland. Their doorways are always high off the ground, as they were used as refuges from attack. Running my hand along its rounded walls I think of my walk ahead and the similar round tower at the other end of St Declan's Way in Ardmore.

As I leave the Rock I ask a couple of the guides standing at the front desk if they know about St Declan's Way. When they look blank I am relieved that I'm turning my back on the seat of Saint Patrick and tracing the steps of his predecessor Declan back to where he is known and revered in Ardmore.

6

Books and bishops

Yesterday when Tom O'Brien heard I was walking St Declan's Way he told me it followed the river out beyond the hostel, but then added inauspiciously that I shouldn't go that way as barely a mile further on it was flooded and impassable. However, when I look at my map I discover it doesn't actually follow the river, but heads through the town and past the Church of Ireland Cathedral. So I turn down John Street and past its Georgian terraced houses with their wide stone steps and fan windows above the different-coloured front doors—one bright fuchsia pink, another crushed raspberry.

When I reach St John's Cathedral I find a flock of sheep grazing among the gravestones. A tractor pulls in, so I ask the driver if they belong to him.

'No,' he says, explaining he is just picking up the leftover soil from his parents' grave. He is not at all happy about the sheep, and mutters something about a Miss Thompson being

27

to blame. Then he points to the wire fence around his parents' grave to protect it from the woolly interlopers, and says that is not the way for a grave to be.

It transpires he does not have much time for the present dean either. He tells me Dean Woodworth, who died about fifteen years ago, was a great man. He passed away while mowing the churchyard. 'He's buried over there,' the man says, pointing towards the far side of the churchyard. He describes how in Dean Woodworth's day he and five other men all worked to keep the church grounds in good order. They used to keep rabbits in hutches for people to look at as they walked around the churchyard, he reminisces, while I ponder this unusual idea.

He is a round man with a thick accent and has a smell of earth and manure about him. His name is Pat Marshall, and he is joint master with his brother of the Cashel Harriers, which his father, who was from Cashel, started 80 years ago. Pat's mother came from the nearby village of Coleraine. His parents met at an all-night dance on the road. Apparently all the local musicians used to meet at a crossroads and people would dance all night. His fingers are too short to play an instrument, he adds, but his nephew who works in the butcher's is a very good musician.

I leave Pat to his soil moving and walk over to the small box-like Georgian building next to the cathedral which houses the Bolton Library. I notice a woman smoking a cigarette outside. This is Pauline Huseby, the assistant librarian, who tells me the Bolton Library holds the smallest book in the world. Only three-sixteenths of an inch square in size, the book has a black cover with a silver cross on it and 24 pages on which is written the Lord's Prayer in German.

'That is certainly not the most interesting book,' says a tall man in his 70s, who appears from nowhere. Initially, I think this must be the new dean, but as he talks animatedly about the library I realise it's Charles Hazell. He and his wife are friends of my mother.

Years ago when I was living in Dublin, Charles and I were taking the same ferry from Dunleary across the Irish Sea to Holyhead. I was always nervous travelling on the ferry, because the Irish Sea can be very rough and many passengers seemed to lack sea legs. They would throw up with the slightest swell, or drink as much as they could at the duty-free bar in as short a time as possible, stagger about legless and then throw up. To avoid these shenanigans I used to spend most of the crossing roaming the decks or sitting in the 'solarium', which at night in winter was extremely cold. Charles introduced me to travelling first class. As an impoverished actress I had never considered such a luxury, but it did not cost much more and I would have paid almost any amount not to be surrounded by people getting legless and throwing up. In first class, I discovered, people did neither and nor did their dogs which travelled first class with them.

Charles used to work at the Bolton Library on a voluntary basis, until he was banned from entering it due to a disagreement with the bishop. As he is not allowed to come into the building, we stand outside while he gives me a potted history of the library, then Pauline shows me around. With its 12 000 books including early manuscripts and some of the first printed books, this library's significance, Charles believes, is on a par with the Rock of Cashel, and should be promoted as such, but apparently the bishop does not agree.

As Charles describes the books, it becomes obvious this little building holds a valuable history of the written word. There are early writings in papyrus, a book of gospels handwritten on vellum, and an encyclopedia printed less than 20 years after the Gutenberg invented the first printing press. There are also here a few pages of William Caxton's printing of Geoffrey Chaucer's *Canterbury Tales*. According to Charles, Caxton was an untidy printer. However, he printed using the English language. At the time this was very unusual and almost dangerous, but as Caxton was a businessman he could afford to do it.

The most valuable book on display is the *Nuremberg Chronicle*, an illustrated history of the world printed in Germany more than 600 years ago. The exquisite detailed illustrations are produced from woodcuts. One of the engravers is believed to be Albrecht Durer. 'This,' Charles says, 'is one of the most famous books ever printed and this is the only one in Ireland.'

In a glass-topped cabinet I find a copy of the bible in Irish. While the Roman Catholic Church service was always given in Latin, many Protestant churches gave the service in Irish and it was the Protestant Church which first translated the bible into Irish. I discover later it was Queen Elizabeth I who first ordered a special typeface be designed based on Irish written letter forms, so religious texts could be made available to the Irish in their native language.

The bible in the Bolton Library was financed by Robert Boyle, the scientist of Boyle's Law renown, who grew up in Lismore Castle. His father, Richard Boyle, bought the castle and land from Sir Walter Raleigh and went on to become one of the largest landowners in Ireland.

If I hadn't bumped into Charles Hazell, I probably would have taken only a quick glance at the books on display. With books so available to most of us, it's easy today to underestimate the power of the written word. But Charles's passion is contagious—and he is right. The Bolton Library is of great significance, and if I were the bishop I would utilise this man's boundless enthusiasm to spread the word.

7

Brigid

On my way out Pauline points out a large stone sheela-na-gig. This 28-inch high female fertility figure was found buried under a yew tree in a graveyard in the nearby village of Clonoulty and is believed to have been carved more than 400 years ago. The face is chipped away, but her small squatting legs can be clearly seen with her right hand holding open her vulva.

Sheela-na-gigs, with their ugly facial features, small withered breasts and huge vulvas, are found in churches and castles all over Ireland. They are believed to provide protection. Most of them are between 1000 and 400 years old, so they are clear evidence of the survival of the goddess in the Christian era.

Sheela-na-gigs are often carved in prominent positions in churches. Sometimes they are above the main porch, so as you go through the arched doorway, you symbolically enter the womb of the goddess. You pass through the gateway to death and regeneration and into the realm of the sacred feminine. The sheela-na-gig is also symbolic of the spiritual power of sexuality. For women to identify with the goddess within them, and men to make love to the goddess in women.

The much-loved Brigid, also called Briget and Bride, is the best example of the continuation of goddess worship. Sometimes she is known as Mary of the Gaels. And myth says she was the Virgin Mary's midwife and Jesus' wet nurse. She is revered today in Ireland as both a goddess and saint.

It is said that a flame in honour of the ancient goddess Brigid burnt in Kildare long before it was first tended by St Brigid and her nuns 1500 years ago when she founded the abbey there. The name Kildare comes from the Irish *cill dara*, which means 'church of the oak'. This echoes earlier beliefs as the Druids believed the oak was sacred. To them the oak tree, which can easily live a thousand years, represented power and protection and was a symbol of inner and outer strength. Interestingly, the oak tree has also always been associated with St Brigid.

Several years ago on our way back from Dublin Stephen and I stopped in Kildare town. In the cathedral grounds we saw the rectangular foundations of what was a fire temple to Brigid. From the pre-Christian era the fire burnt continuously for centuries until a bishop decided it should be extinguished as it was too pagan. After his death the fire was relit and burnt until the sixteenth century, when the abbey was disbanded.

While we were there I visited the Christian centre for St Brigid and Celtic spirituality called Solas Bhríde, which means 'flame of Brigid'. Founded by two Brigidine nuns twenty years ago it was set up to teach people about the legacy of St Brigid and its relevance today. It also reconnects with the values and wisdom of Celtic spirituality and fully acknowledges the goddess aspect of Brigid.

The Solas Bhríde centre is in a modern house near the centre of town, which is also the two nuns' home, and pilgrims come here from all over the world. In the main room there's a shrine swathed in rainbow coloured material. Standing on it is a lantern and inside burns the perpetual flame of Brigid, which was relit here in 1993.

There is also a beautiful icon of St Brigid holding a symbol of her abbey in her hand. One foot stands on her father's sword which she gave away. Her father Dubthach was an Irish chieftain. Believing that Brigid would make the family destitute because she gave so much to the poor, he decided to sell her to the king. Dubthach left Brigid in his chariot while he spoke to the king and along came a poor man needing bread to feed his family. All Brigid could give to the man was her father's precious sword, so she did. Her father was extremely angry when he returned and discovered what she had done, and was keener than ever to sell her, but the king, realising the special qualities of this girl, said she should never be sold.

Behind Brigid in the icon her blue cloak stretches over the flat plains of the Curragh. Brigid approached the King of Leinster to procure land for her abbey. Not wanting to give away his land the king said he would give her as much land as her cloak would cover. Miraculously, when she laid out her cloak it stretched over the Curragh, 5000 acres of flat grassland, and so Brigid had all the land she needed. Today the Curragh is still common grazing land, and that right originated with Brigid.

'It is impossible to separate Saint Brigid from the Celtic goddess, Brigid,' Sister Phil O'Shea, one of the centre's founders, told me. 'The two are so interwoven.'

In Celtic mythology Brigid was the triple goddess—the maiden, the mother and the crone. She was also the goddess of the four elements—air, fire, water and earth—from which life is made and sustained.

One lovely age-old tradition, which continues in Ireland today, is to make Brigid crosses to protect the home and hearth. These crosses are made from woven rushes, and shaped like a swastika. For the ancient Celts these crosses symbolised the four directions and the four elements.

Kieran Heffernan, a family friend, told me how when he was young his family used to hang these crosses up on St Brigid's Day, February 1, to bring good fortune to their home for the year. The crosses were then burnt on the eve of St Brigid's Day the following year, and new ones were made and hung up. Kieran also recounted how he and his father would place their ties on their bedroom windowsills before going to bed on the eve of St Brigid's Day. His sister and mother would do the same with a scarf or a ribbon, to be blessed and safeguarded by the saint through the year ahead.

St Brigid's Day shows how Christian beliefs and Celtic traditions have merged. It is also the day of Imbolc, the fire festival midway between the winter solstice and spring equinox in the pagan calendar in the northern hemisphere, and the day of the Goddess Brigid.

Many wells and springs in Ireland are dedicated to Brigid and believed to have the power to heal, and at this time of year people would also tie pieces of material to trees beside them. The belief is that as the material disintegrates with the wind and the rain during the year, the fear, worry or perhaps illness that has been plaguing you also disappears. John Walsh, our neighbour at Camphire Hill, told me how the spring in the corner of his field used to be visited by all the locals at Imbolc when he was a child and pieces of material were tied to the tree beside it. This tradition continues today.

At St Brigid's Well and Prayer Stones, which I visited when I was in Kildare, the long branches of the slender tree beside the well were festooned with pieces of material. High up a black and white spotted dress swung in the breeze. A blue dish cloth was tied to one branch alongside different coloured handkerchiefs. There were also ties and ribbons and rags blowing in the wind. It was a wonderful celebration of the sacred in everyday life.

I always try to celebrate the pagan sacred wheel of the year with its summer and winter solstices, two equinoxes and four crossquarter fire festivals. I may just light a candle, give thanks for the year so far and think about what's ahead, as well as acknowledging the changing seasons. It's a simple ritual, but it's these moments that allow me to honour the traditions that come before me. I am drawn to the strong Celtic connection with nature and I hope a better understanding of that will be one of the gifts of walking St Declan's Way.

I leave the Bolton Library and return to the hostel. There is a tripod set up in the middle of the kitchen and two Austrian men in their twenties called Wolfgang and Michael are cooking supper. They have driven around Ireland in a week. Most nights they have slept in their hire car and are keeping a blog of the trip. Wolfgang's father is a butcher and he gives me a piece of the salami-like sausage his father has made. Wolfgang explains that he is a photographer and when he hears about my pilgrimage he offers to take a photograph of me in front of the Rock of Cashel in the morning.

Once Wolfgang and Michael turn in for the night, I sit at a table writing my journal. A young couple come in, introduce themselves as Andrew and Lauren and set up a laptop at another table. Lauren taps away, while Andrew writes his diary. Andrew and Lauren are both Australians at university in Scotland for a year. As they are too young to hire a car, they came over to Ireland from England on the ferry and are travelling around on buses. Lauren's grandmother was a Maher whose family graves are up on the Rock.

They were in Waterford city the previous night, and went to a pub with live music. Lauren says all the old people there got up and danced, and were obviously having a great time. She talks wistfully of the happiness she saw in such a simple pleasure. It becomes obvious she is entranced by what she had seen of Ireland so far, as she chatters with unfettered enthusiasm about the country and its people.

I understand her rosy-tinted view of Ireland. She is looking in on a world that she never had, and yearning for what she feels her generation has lost. Whoever in her family decided to emigrate to the other side of the world did not make that decision lightly. There's little doubt that it would have been to make a better life, but in so doing there would be essential aspects of their existence they would never experience again.

As I listen to Lauren's yearning for a different way in life, I recognise in me that desire to belong to a community that doesn't sit night after night in front of a television, but sings, dances and plays music together in the evenings. I, too, ache to belong to a people that have a history on their land.

8

Raths and a heavy backpack

The following morning Wolfgang sets his tripod up beside the road, while Michael holds various pieces of equipment. I am delighted to have a photograph of me in front of the Rock. It'll be evidence at least that I set off from Cashel. I imagine it's going to be a couple of clicks and all over, until I realise that Wolfgang is an artist. He is determined to capture the best light from the grey sky, so keeps reading the light meter before adjusting the lens and then the tripod. He is now positioned in the middle of the road, but every minute or so a car comes speeding along, so he has to quickly get his tripod and himself out of the way. As I start to wish I'd given at least some attention to my appearance and perhaps applied some lipstick, the picture is finally taken.

By the time I've emptied and repacked my backpack it's 11 a.m when I finally leave for Cahir, moaning to Tom O'Brien about the weight of my pack. Unsympathetic, he tells me that I should have done at least three days walking with it before setting out, and also left earlier this morning. Luckily Stephen is not at home when I ring him from the telephone box on the main street. I know he would tell me I should have left before now, too. What makes it worse is they're probably both right.

I head down John Street past the cathedral and south along what is, according to Tom O'Brien, known locally as the 'old road'. As I walk up the hill towards the school straight ahead of me, I just make out in the far distance the saddle-shaped dip of Bottleneck Pass on the Knockmealdown Mountains. I'll be walking over the mountains in a few days time. I turn around to look at the Rock of Cashel one last time. To my surprise the Rock is not visible from here, but immediately ahead in the far distance is the Devil's Bit. Then I realise this is the exact spot that Christopher Horsman told me about.

When I told friends I was walking St Declan's Way, several people suggested I contact Christopher because he had also walked it. We spoke on the telephone a couple of weeks ago and he told me about this stretch of road. He believes that because the road runs between the two distinctive landmarks of the Devil's Gap and Bottleneck Pass it is in fact an ancient highway that pre-dates St Declan. Yet again the different layers of history are apparent.

The town quickly gives away to the countryside. White bindweed with its trumpet-like flowers crowns the top of the hedges. Below it are the little pink flowers of herb Robert and purple vetch. I find blackberries growing in the hedges, too, but when I put them in my mouth they are sour and watery.

According to the map I just follow this quiet country road, but after a mile and a half it leads onto the busy N8 road near the motorway. So I ask directions from a woman standing in her garden. She explains that I need to cross the bridge over the motorway and join the old road again on the other side of it. She also says there is a rath a little further down the main road.

Apparently these circular enclosures with their earth banks were originally Iron Age forts. The raths used to have huts inside them and were used between 500 and 1500 years ago. However, they are also known as fairy forts, as fairies and leprechauns are believed to live in them. For that reason they have been left undisturbed, as it is thought to be very bad luck to interfere with them. The fairies who live in raths are called *aes sídhe*, fairies of the mound. They love music and dancing, and come out at night to party.

It's believed that the fairies were originally the gods or *Tuatha Dé Danann*, who came into Ireland enshrouded by a magical mist. This strange mist obscured them and the sun for three days and three nights, which gave them enough time to use their supernatural skills to take over the country from its former inhabitants, the Fomors. Shortly after the *Tuatha Dé Danann* established themselves in Ireland, the sons of Mil, the Milesian race from which the Irish today are descended, attacked them. Although initially the Milesians were defeated by the gods' magic, the mortal race finally won. They made an agreement with the gods that they would inhabit the earth's surface, and the gods would live in the bowels of the earth and the sea caves. And so this is how the *Tuatha Dé Danann* became known as the 'little people'.

The belief in spirits and other beings, which has been lost in much of the modern world, is still evident in Ireland. Today, very few people have the ability to see fairies, but there are still reports of them being heard or seen.

Although fairies are often kind, they can get angry or be mischievous, so even now people are wary of upsetting them. Major highways in Ireland have been rerouted around fairy locations. Ten years ago the *New York Times* ran a story about a hawthorn bush near Latoon, a village in the west of Ireland, that was to be bulldozed to make way for a bypass around a nearby town. Eddie Lenehan, a traditional storyteller, warned that if the bush was bulldozed the fairies could wreak havoc on the new road, causing brakes to fail and cars to crash. A local farmer had seen white fairy blood around the bush, which indicated that this hawthorn was a favourite meeting place for the little people. So the bypass was diverted and the town planners even put a wooden fence around the hawthorn to protect it.

As I walk along the busy road I see a circle of trees up on the hill, and assume that must be the rath. But there is a large sign saying 'Private Property No Entry' on the gate into the field leading up to it, so I decide not to check it out.

Retracing my steps and heading towards the motorway I remember the story of the great Irish bard, Turlough O'Carolan. It is said he slept one night in a fairy rath, and was able to sing and play fairy tunes on his harp from then on. Born more than 300 years ago O'Carolan was blinded by smallpox at eighteen and apprenticed to a harper. At 21 he was given a horse and a guide and, for the next 50 years he travelled around Ireland composing songs and music and performing to enthusiastic audiences. Today more than 200 tunes are accredited to him.

A mile or so along the old road, according to the map, I am near the large and poetically named *Rath na Drinna*, Rath of the Blackthorns. On the hill to the left is a clump of bushes, indicating where the rath lies. Eager to take a closer look I find again the gates up to the rath have large notices warning people off. Not game to trespass, I move on. A few days later I discover why farmers do not want people looking at the raths on their land—it's the curse of public liability.

I haven't walked far from the rath when I decide I need a break. I take off my backpack and sink onto the grass beside the road, feeling utter relief to get the weight off my back. It's almost one o'clock so I eat my lunch. I'm frustrated that I haven't been able to see either of the two raths and my shoulders hurt. Then I look at the map and realise I have only walked two and a half miles and it is another nine to Cahir.

I have never carried a backpack before, apart from the morning a couple of weeks ago when I did a test run with my friend Teresa, who lent it to me. I packed everything the night before we met. I felt very apprehensive about my pack-carrying ability and also a little nauseous. I wondered if the physical exertion of carrying this backpack was going to be similar to when another friend, who I later discovered was one of Hong Kong's top female mountain bikers, took me cycling up the Peak, Hong Kong Island's highest mountain, in 97 per cent humidity, and I threw up.

The following morning I staggered slowly under my burden up the hill to meet Teresa. When I told her how hideously heavy the backpack felt, she assured me I would get used to it. We walked up and down steps, along a beach, on dirt paths and over rocks, stopping occasionally to admire the view or for a snack, concluding with lunch in a café. By the time I got home I had walked about nine miles and was still standing, so decided I would be fine ambling along St Declan's Way.

Though I only have to cover the same distance as the test run and largely on the flat, I wonder if I am even going to make it to Cahir today. It does cross my mind that I could limp back to Cashel and rethink this whole journey. But then I notice a place on the map called Newinn, halfway to Cahir, and decide that if worst comes to worst I can spend the night there.

9

good boots

More relaxed now I settle into the afternoon's walking. Honeysuckle, with its yellowy-pink flowers, weaves through the hedges on either side of the narrow road. I pass a bank of meadowsweet, the plant of the moon goddess Áine, protector of women and goddess of love and fertility. It's to her that the cream-coloured flowers of meadowsweet, the plant considered so sacred by the druids, owe their seductive scent. It is said Áine appears on the eve of the summer solstice. Bonfires used to burn all night in her honour, as the bringer of good harvest and fine cattle.

Until now I have been walking along narrow roads with high hedges. But the road opens up at this point and I stroll alongside a wide grass verge. Beside me in a field are two thoroughbred mares, each with a foal. I stand at the gate hoping they will come to me. After much neighing between them, eventually one approaches and allows her nose to be stroked. As I feel the warm air from her nostrils on my hand,

I realise how lucky I am to have the time in the day for this moment. Then as I continue walking down the road both the mares and their foals start galloping beside me and I feel even more fortunate.

At a jagged crossroads, to my great excitement, I see a brown metal sign pointing back the way I have come, saying '*Slí Naomh Deagláin* St Declan's Way Cashel'. It's only a small detail, but a wonderful confirmation that the way is a recognised route.

Actually, from Cashel to south of Lismore, some 34 miles down the track, St Declan's Way is also known by the far less glamorous name of *Rian Bó Pádraig*, the Way of Patrick's Cow. Apparently, St Patrick's cow was grazing peacefully with her calf when the calf was abducted by a cattle-thief. The robber headed home to Kilwatermoy, south of the Bride River near Lismore, with the calf, and when the cow discovered her loss she followed in hot pursuit. In her fury she tore up the earth with her horns as she went, making a double trench, until she caught up with the robber and gave him what for.

An hour and a half later I reach the turning to Newinn. Spurred on by the realisation that I am halfway to Cahir, I press on to Ballygerald churchyard, just a little further down the road. Around the ruined church are scattered a couple of large tombs and rows of headstones. A white marble cross lies forgotten beside the crumbling stone wall of the church and nearby an Irish yew with its red berries stands like a sentinel guarding the dead. For the Irish Celts the yew symbolised life and death. They used yew wood to make bows and a compound of yew berries to poison their arrows.

I lie down on a low foundation wall of what was once the church. The relief of stretching my back and resting my feet is bliss. After about fifteen minutes, I decide to do some yoga. I kneel on the wall with my eyes closed, exhaling and inhaling loudly while throwing my arms into the air. Then I open my eyes to see a couple with ashen grey faces heading to a nearby grave. All I can hope is that they don't think my gesticulations are part of some sort of satanic ritual.

I have been trying not to focus on the pain in my left little toe, but now I take off my boot and see that underneath the nail is purple. It's not a great start to the walk, but having no remedy, I put my boot back on and just try to forget about it.

I am still only half way to Cahir and it is after 4 p.m. so I realise I need to pick up the pace. Looking at the map I notice some dots going across country rather than by the road. This shortcut would probably save me more than half a mile, so I decide to take it. It looks as if the path runs alongside the driveway down to Lough Kent, and I turn down the drive to look for it. I reach a stableyard to find two horses, their heads hanging over their stable doors, listening to Van Morrison on the radio. I am unable to find the path or anyone to ask about it. So, having probably walked an extra mile and a half, I have little choice but to retrace my steps back to the road. Later, when studying the map in more detail, I discover that the widely spaced dots I was looking at do not indicate a path at all, but the probable original route. Another lesson—read the map more carefully.

A scattering of houses either side of the road indicates the townland of Mortlestown. A townland sounds like an impressive place, but there are more than 60 000 of them in Ireland, and their size varies according to the fertility of the land. They are an old Gaelic system of land division originally and although usually several hundred acres, they can also be as small as a single acre.

Nearly 200 years ago a man from Mortlestown who had seven sons and was known by the name of Costigan removed half of a rath. He became ill and the doctor in Cahir could not cure him. So his family went to another doctor. This second doctor gave Costigan's seven sons a bottle of medicine, and said if they could take it home to their father it would cure him. It broke several miles from home, and the same thing happened with a second bottle. On the third attempt they got the bottle home in one piece, but arrived to find their father was dead.

The next stretch is along a very busy road. Every time two cars pass me simultaneously I have to stand in the ditch. So I am pleased when I turn onto a narrow back road with a strip of grass up the middle. A woman gives me a friendly wave from her front door, and calls back her black and white collie, Max, who looks as if he would like to take a nip at my ankles. Further on the road passes through a farmyard and beyond that I pass two fields of wheat. The heads are tired and blackish. Presumably the opportunity to harvest the crop has been lost with all the rain. It makes me realise how easy it is living in a city to forget that we rely on the fertile ground and good weather for our food.

Men on tractors speed up and down the road and children play in the front gardens of houses beside the road. Suddenly I feel as if I have been stripped of my identity. These people are going about their daily lives. They belong here on this land, but I feel like a fish out of water. I am not part of this world, only walking through with a pack on my back. So what does it mean to belong? It's a question I often ask myself. I also wonder whether the large numbers of Eastern Europeans who have come to Ireland for work over the last few years feel as if they belong here. Then I think of all the Irish over the years who have emigrated to places like England, America and Australia for economic reasons, and how often they are torn between their new home and Ireland.

This elusive state of belonging that I've been chasing for so much of my life is like a pot of gold at the foot of a rainbow. In this moment I desperately want to belong, and yet I have no desire to live in this rural community along this particular road, because I have no connection to this place. Then I have a moment of clarity. I have always thought belonging could only come from acceptance by other people and their acknowledgement, but in the end the sense of belonging I so often crave can only come from within me. It's very comforting to realise that it isn't about trying to fit in—something I've wasted a lot of my life doing—but rather about making connections, which can be done in myriad different ways.

My epiphany is followed by a particularly sharp bolt of pain shooting through my toe. It's painful every time my left foot hits the ground, so I have begun to limp. Maybe that is why an old man stops his car and, looking very concerned, asks if I'm all right.

There two more raths marked on the map, but as I can't see them from the road and with a fair distance still to Cahir, I don't bother to look for them. Now I'm focused on my destination. Yet as I walk down a hill I can't help stopping to admire a picture-book farm with whitewashed old buildings and a bed of magnificent orange marigolds in front of its white walls. Across the valley a ray of sunlight pierces the low grey cloud hanging over the rounded tops of the Galtee Mountains.

At the bottom of the hill is the main road into Cahir and there are two brown metal signs pointing in opposite directions. In white letters is written 'St Declan's Way Cashel' on one and 'St Declan's Way Ardmore' on the other. My heart leaps to see this. Up until now I thought that the Way was meant to be walked from Ardmore to Cashel, but this sign is validation that it's okay to walk from Cashel to Ardmore, too.

So I hobble happily past an old disused mill and into Cahir. I ring the doorbell of the house opposite the post office, from which accommodation at the town's only hostel is organised. No one comes to the door. So I take down the telephone number on the faded sign and ring it from the telephone box across the road. A woman answers immediately and tells me the Lisakyle Hostel is several miles out of town and to phone again when I am ready to go there and her husband will drive me.

I pause for a moment. What to do? I decided when planning to walk St Declan's Way that I would not accept lifts, but here I am at the end of day one barely able to walk 30 yards from the telephone box to the pub beyond it. The idea of another 2 miles is unthinkable.

I step slowly and gingerly along the street to the Galtee Inn, and sit at a large round table near the door, feeling utterly spent. I look at my watch. It's quarter to eight and the first leg of the Way is complete. A man droops with drink across the end of the long bar, while the barman orders him a taxi. Half a dozen people are sitting at a table out the front smoking. Soul music is playing loudly in the back bar for the stragglers of a wedding party.

A middle-aged Lithuanian woman, who tells me she has lived in Cahir for the last four years, pours me a glass of Guinness then brings me a vegetarian dish made from local Baylough cheese which is named after the mysterious black lake on the Knockmealdowns. She also places a huge bowl of potatoes on the table, something which apparently accompanies all the meals. With the tiredness now spreading right through my body I'm not able to make much of a dent on all the food and only manage to eat two potatoes. My feet are screaming not to be walked on. Even though the pilgrim part of me protests, I decide to accept the lift to the hostel.

As Maurice Conlon, who is in his 70s, drives me out of town he tells me that 'You need good boooots, not shoes, for walking'. When I ask if he does much walking himself, he says he used to walk behind the horses and the plough, but that was 40 years ago. He hasn't much time for men sitting on tractors all day complaining they are tired, he adds.

We arrive at an old farmhouse covered in a deep red-coloured ivy. Inside the place looks almost unchanged since the 1950s. In the main room a young French couple are sitting at a wooden table eating supper, the man with his eye on a game of football on the television. Behind them is a large dresser with a row of plates on the top. There are two wooden armchairs upholstered in a pink material, which has worn on the arms. In the fireplace a vase of orange montbretia flowers has been placed on a wooden box. Above it are the old black iron hooks for hanging cooking pots over the fire, and in a wall recess next to the fireplace is a wheel you turn to draw the fire.

Maurice leads me up the narrow staircase with its brown patterned carpet into a room with four bunk beds. When he leaves I go downstairs to the kitchen to make myself a mug of tea. The cooker is an old four-burner gas top. Next to it is a large high-tech new toaster. There are two white plastic kettles. Both are filthy. I finally find a mug that is neither chipped or without a handle. On the draining board is a packet of dog biscuits and a tin of dog food, and in the middle of the floor a large bowl, but no sign of a dog.

I choose the least grubby of the two bathrooms to wash in, swap a nylon pillowcase for a cotton one and clamber up into the corner top bunk. The whole framework sways like a ship in rolling waves. Then I notice the bed base is made from chipboard. I wonder if Maurice has knocked up these bunk beds himself. To add insult to injury this costs the same as the beautiful clean O'Brien Cashel Lodge I left this morning. I go to sleep deciding that, pilgrim or no pilgrim and regardless of the cost, my next night will definitely be spent in a luxurious bed and breakfast.

10

The Legend of Knockgrafton

Nine hours later I wake up still stiff and tired, but my feet no longer ache like they did last night. I take a blanket off one of the beds, spread it on the floor and do some yoga stretches in the hope of easing my stiff muscles. Half an hour later I go downstairs to find a man with an unkempt mop of grey hair who looks like an Irish farmer. His wife is in the kitchen cooking breakfast. They introduce themselves as Bernard and Debby, the owners of Jay Jay, a large black standard poodle, whose bowl and biscuits I found last night. Debby offers me a bowl of porridge and we sit around the wooden table while Jay Jay sleeps stretched out in the middle of the room.

They have been staying in the master bedroom which has an ensuite, Debby tells me, though, she adds, the bathroom floor is covered in slugs at night as they sliver in under the outside door. Bernard's mother was a Grogan, one of eight children from the nearby Glen of Aherlow. She trained as a nurse, moved to England and married an Englishman. Because of rationing in England after the war, as a boy Bernard was sent back to the farm in Ireland every school holidays. Debby and he now come every year to visit his relations. He has a number of elderly aunts in nursing homes, and when he first arrives he always goes to the graveyard, so he can see who has died.

It was in the Glen of Aherlow at the foot of the Galtee Mountains that a humpbacked man once lived, so the Legend of Knockgrafton goes. The Legend of Knockgrafton was first recorded by Thomas Crofton Croker, a collector of Irish songs and legends. He included the story in his book, *Fairy Legends and Traditions of the South of Ireland* which was published in 1826, and this is a slightly shorter version of the original tale.

The poor man had such a great lump on his back he looked as if his body had been rolled up and placed on his shoulders. He was known as Lusmore because he always wore a sprig of the fairy cap, the foxglove or *lus mór* in Irish, in his little straw hat.

One evening Lusmore was returning from Cahir, and because of the great hump on his back he was walking very slowly. It was dark when he came to the old mound known as the motte of Knockgrafton. He was very tired and worried about how much further he had to travel to his home in Cappagh.

He sat down by the motte to rest, and as he gazed at the moon he heard a melody. It was like the sound of many voices, but each blending and mingling with the others so they seemed to be one. The words of the song were, 'Da Luan, Da Mort, Da Luan, Da Mort, Da Luan, Da Mort, Da Luan, Da Mort,'—'Da Luan' meaning Monday and 'Da Mort', Tuesday—after which there was a moment's pause and the melody would start again.

Lusmore realised the singing was coming from the motte. Initially the sound charmed him, but then he began to get tired of hearing the same round sung again and again, so next time the singing paused he took up the tune with the words 'augus Da Dardeen'—'and Wednesday too'.

When the fairies singing the tune heard this addition they were so delighted they decided to bring the mortal who sang it into their company. Little Lusmore was whisked down through the motte, into a great hall. There he was given the great honour of being put above all the fairy musicians, tended to by servants and treated like a king. But then he noticed the fairies were consulting among themselves, and although they had been most civil, he felt very frightened. Eventually, one fairy stepped away from the rest and said:

Lusmore! Lusmore!
Doubt not, nor deplore,
For the hump which you bore
On your back is no more;
Look down on the floor,
And view it, Lusmore.

With these words Lusmore saw his hump tumble down from his shoulders onto the ground. Overpowered by the scene his eyesight dimmed and he fell into a deep sleep.

When Lusmore woke up it was daylight and he found himself lying at the foot of Knockgrafton. The first thing he did, after saying his prayers, was to feel for his hump, but it wasn't there. He was also wearing a suit of new clothes.

He walked home but no one who saw Lusmore knew him without his hump, and he had trouble persuading everyone he was the same man. Before long though, the story of Lusmore's hump got about, and it was the talk of the country for miles around.

One morning Lusmore was sitting at his cabin door when an old woman stopped to ask if he could help her. 'I have come out of Déise country, from the county of Waterford,' the woman said, 'looking for one Lusmore who I have heard had his hump taken off by the fairies.' She explained that the son of a friend of hers had a hump on him, and maybe if he could use the same charm as Lusmore the hump could be taken off him.

Lusmore, who was a good-natured little fellow, told the woman how he had completed the fairies' melody at Knockgrafton and how his hump had been removed and he had also got a new suit of clothes into the bargain.

The woman thanked him and went home to her friend and told her everything Lusmore had said, and they put the little humpbacked man, Jack Madden, who was a peevish and cunning creature from his birth, in a cart and took him all the way to Knockgrafton where they left him at night fall.

Jack Madden had not been sitting there long before he heard the fairies' tune in the motte.

He was in a great hurry to get rid of his hump, and he never thought of waiting until the fairies were done, or listening for an opportunity to improve the melody. So, having heard them sing it seven times without stopping, he bawled 'augus Da Dardeen, augus Da Hena'—'and Wednesday and Thursday too'—thinking to himself that if Lusmore had one suit of clothes given to him, why shouldn't he have two?

No sooner than the words passed his lips he was whisked into the motte, and the fairies came crowding round him in great anger, screeching and screaming, 'Who spoilt our tune? Who spoilt our tune?' Then one stepped out from the rest and said:

Jack Madden! Jack Madden!
Your words came so bad in
The tune we felt glad in;
This castle you're had in,
That your life we may sadden;
Here's two humps for Jack Madden!

Then twenty of the strongest fairies brought Lusmore's hump and put it down over Jack's own hump, where it became as firmly fixed as if it was nailed on by the best carpenter. The fairies kicked him out of the motte and the next morning when Jack's mother and her friend came to look for him, they found him half-dead with another hump on his back. Terrified to say anything in case a hump might be put on their shoulders too, they brought him home. But with the weight of the second hump and the long journey Jack died soon after, leaving, they say, his heavy curse to anyone who would to listen to fairy tunes again.

11

The kindness of strangers

Bernard and Debby are catching the ferry back to England today, but meeting them warms me to Lisakyle Hostel, so I decide to spend another night here. I always planned to spend two nights in Cahir to give myself time to look around the town and visit its castle, and the Swiss Cottage, the exquisite cottage orné that I've heard about but never seen. I'm in the bathroom washing the socks, knickers and shirt that I wore yesterday when I notice the grey cloud, which has cloaked the sky ever since I arrived in Ireland, has lifted.

'The sun is out,' I blurt with excitement.

'And the daughter will be out in a moment, too,' Maurice replies solemnly from the kitchen. He is removing hundreds of tiny black bugs from a lampshade, supposedly caused by Bernard and Debby leaving their bedroom light on last night.

I leave him to his chores and get a lift with the French couple into Cahir.

When I ring Stephen and tell him about my crippling experience yesterday, he replies that soldiers on the march always take great care of their feet, and suggests I do the same. So I go to a chemist and buy some nail scissors and a packet of plasters for blisters. Walking along the bank of the River Suir, past three men sitting on the ground swigging large bottles of cider, I find a suitable solitary spot for performing a pedicure.

As I sit on the grass cutting my toenails and applying a plaster to my little toe I think of Miguel and Baptista, the two Spanish walkers my cousin Carolyn and I befriended when we were cycling along the Camino de Santiago in the north of Spain.

Carolyn and I spent much of our days lying in fields, picnicking beside the road, sitting in bars, or sketching and writing our diaries. In between our many stops we cycled very slowly, so we were travelling at the same pace as fellow foot pilgrims, Miguel and Baptista, for about a week. They used to limp into the *refugios*, the pilgrim refuges along the Camino, at the end of the day under the weight of their large heavy backpacks then go through a ritual of foot therapy. First they put their aching feet in a bucket of warm water mixed with bicarbonate of soda before dressing their large raw blisters in preparation for more walking the following day. At times their faces scrunched up with the pain, but regardless of the agony they were always cheerful.

The last time we saw Miguel and Baptista was on our way up the Montes de Léon. Despite being mid-spring it began to snow as Carolyn and I cycled slowly up the winding road. The mountain became a blanket of white. We sheltered at the top of the pass in a deserted stone building. Carolyn's hands were so numb with cold I had to rub the circulation back into them. At the next town we went in search of gloves, but were only able to find extra large yellow gardening gloves. In desperation we bought those and were very grateful for them when two days later we were snowed in at a mountain village called Cebreiro.

Not realising there were pilgrim refuges all along the Camino, and expecting to stay in little local hotels, we had no sleeping bags. Luckily we had always found blankets to cover ourselves at night. But on this freezing night, as huge white snow flakes fell silently outside and with the temperature steadily dropping, there was not one blanket to be found.

Carolyn and I put on every single item of clothing we were carrying. I lay on the mattress, wearing my shorts over my trousers, with a beret on my head and the yellow gardening gloves on my feet, exhausted and too cold to sleep. We looked so pathetic that the two Spanish teachers sharing the room with us gave us one of their sleeping bags. Carolyn and I huddled together in a narrow single bunk bed, our bodies pressed together and the sleeping bag over us until finally we were warm enough to sleep. Oh, the kindness of strangers.

A week earlier a pilgrim we met briefly on the road gave us 2000 pesetas because we had not realised the banks were closed on Saturday. Although we had Visa cards and traveller's cheques, we had no cash. That money was just enough for essentials until Monday morning. We asked the man for his address so we could repay him, but he refused to give it to us, saying, 'This is the way of the Camino'.

Five hundred kilometres later and after three weeks of cycling along tracks and quiet country roads, through towns and villages where stork nests balanced on the roofs of narrow church steeples, over rushing steams and across mountains covered in wild lavender, I felt so proud when our names were read out at the daily mass in the cathedral in Santiago de Compostela. Our slow progress across northern Spain and interactions with fellow pilgrims changed something within us both. Those long days outdoors created a magic which I still don't understand, but I know that cycling the Camino de Santiago was an inspiration for this pilgrimage. I wonder if I'll meet any fellow pilgrims along St Declan's Way.

From the river I walk up to St Paul's, the Protestant church with its impressive spire and steeple. This great Gothic structure was designed by architect John Nash, who constructed the Royal Pavilion in Brighton with its ornate minarets and Indian-style domes. However, the church is locked. I knock on the door of Mrs Hanrahan, who lives across the street and has a key, but she isn't home.

Shut out of the Church of Ireland, I wander down the hill and through the main square with its pretty terraced Georgian houses to the Catholic church. St Mary's is a grey stone building with a high tower. Its doors are open, but inside I am alone. I light a candle, before walking around the modern open plan interior. In a small chapel at the back of the church I find a painting of the virgin and child. Next to it is a small picture of a black Virgin Mary from Czechoslovakia. I imagine one of the many Czech immigrants who are now working in Ireland in the pubs and hotels has found great solace in this little corner.

I'm always drawn to Catholic churches because of the veneration of Mother Mary. I love the lighting of candles, and the combination of intention and the simple ritual. But my joy at doing so is always tempered with an irrational fear that someone in the church will discover I am not a true believer and turf me out.

It is only eleven o'clock and I really need coffee, so I walk back to the Lazy Bean Café in the square, and spend the rest of the morning sitting in the sun, writing my journal and waving wasps off a large cappuccino. At the next table are a group of mothers, also warding off wasps, marvelling at the sunny day—the first, they say, all summer. Ironically it is also their children's first day back at school after the holidays. Here's to hoping the fine weather will hold.

12

The cottage and the well

The day is slipping away so I make my way to the Swiss Cottage, a 200-year-old cottage orné originally designed by John Nash as a rural hideaway for Richard Butler. I walk alongside the river through an avenue of sycamore and horse chestnuts. The long branches of a large oak tree stretch over the water. From the cover of ivy on the ground push up the bright red berries of lords and ladies. The roots of this plant mixed with cow's milk were said to be a remedy for freckles and blemishes of the skin. Above me bunches of dark red elderberries hang down in clusters, reminding me of the elderberry wine that my parents used to make. They poured it into large glass flagons and left it in the warmth of the airing cupboard to ferment. Then at Christmas we'd have a mulled wine party. My father Paul would the play the piano while some of us children accompanied him on flutes and recorders, and everyone else blasted out the carols.

The Swiss Cottage looks like a fairytale home with its undulating thatched roof, delicate French windows opening onto balconies and covered verandahs. With these elaborate touches and the beautifully designed rose-covered trellises, it bears no resemblance to the simplicity of a traditional Irish cottage with thick whitewashed walls and small windows.

When James Butler, the ninth Baron Caher, died, his title and estate went first to his brother, who died two years later in Paris, and then to a cousin who also promptly died. So then the title passed to Richard, his illegitimate son, who was only twelve years old and living in abject poverty with his mother and sister in Cahir. Unaware of his newfound status, Richard was bundled off with his sister to France by relatives who hoped to get their hands on some of the inheritance.

A Mrs Jefferies, the sister of Lord Fitzgibbon, the Chancellor of Ireland, was told this story while spending a night at the inn in Cahir. She sent for the mother of the children and heard her story. When it was found that she was telling the truth, the children were rescued from France, where apparently they were living 'in a garret all overgrown with hair'.

Mrs Jefferies educated the two children and very astutely matched up Richard, now Lord Caher, with her youngest daughter, Emily. They married in London when he was seventeen and she was sixteen, then came to Ireland, and took his mother out of her poverty-stricken existence to enjoy her new status as the Dowager Lady Caher and live with them in comfort.

The inside of the cottage is by tour only and the next one isn't for half an hour, so I climb up the sloping lawn to sit in the sun and wait. Nearby a woman is sitting on the grass reading to her five children, until the smallest boy, who has a crop of bright red hair, starts to chase one of his brothers around the house. Then the youngest girl decides to climb the huge yew tree beside the cottage and is promptly followed by her three brothers.

Yew trees are often planted in churchyards; however, as they can live as long as 5000 years, many specimens pre-date Christianity. Where the Swiss Cottage stands is the site of a monastery, and this magnificent tree is more than 1000 years old. As I watch the children at play I wonder what it has seen in its long lifetime.

This family and I are the only people on the tour. The father in his tailored trousers and his wife in her long navy skirt look wonderfully old-fashioned. She tells me they come from a place which sounds like Cabbage in south Dublin. Her husband's family is from a village near Cahir. They are here on holidays.

First the guide leads us upstairs to the two bedrooms nestled under the eaves, and then shows us the two downstairs rooms, finishing in the most impressive Dufour Room. Its exquisite Rives du Bosphore wallpaper depicts domes and minarets and scenes from Turkish life, and has been restored at great effort and expense. As we stand in the middle of the room, the two girls and eldest boy stare fixedly at me through their metal-rimmed glasses, while the two younger boys pick their noses and look as if they are about to rub their grubby hands all along the walls, or bounce up and down on the delicate Georgian chairs. Their mother and the guide repeat the words 'Don't touch' over and over again.

Leaving the Swiss Cottage I walk back along the river to the Cahir Castle. Built on the rocky island in the middle of the River Suir, it's one of the best preserved Norman castles in Ireland and boasts a working portcullis. It was granted to the Butler family in the fourteenth century and remained in their possession for the next 600 years. As I gallop up and down its narrow stone staircases, it's easy to imagine this fortification full of soldiers clanking around in their chain mail.

Leaving the castle I buy a book on Cahir and discover there is an ancient well about a mile and a half from here. I really want to look at it, but as it is now getting late I'm not sure I can walk there and back before dark. I'm wandering up the main street trying to decide what to do when I notice a man I saw earlier at the castle. He is obviously alone and looks an amiable sort of person so on the spur of the moment I ask him if he wants to go and see the well. After his initial surprise he agrees to drive me there and tells me his name is Jeremy Hicks.

Jeremy is English and works for an industrial laundry business. When he was young, he was run over by a double-decker bus and was extraordinarily lucky not to be killed. This incident made him determined to live life to the full. His job means he travels all over the world and, wherever he is, he tries to see something of the place. So he never stays in the soulless, modern hotels which his company usually books, preferring to find somewhere more interesting, like Cahir House where he is currently staying. It's a magnificent Georgian edifice in the main square built by the Butler family. Since it became a hotel nearly 90 years ago it has accommodated esteemed guests such as Walt Disney and Jackie Kennedy.

We drive out of the town along the Tipperary Road. There is no signpost, but opposite a modern-looking hotel called the Wishing Well is a boreen. A boreen is a narrow, usually unpaved, dirt road. The term comes from the Irish *bóithrín* meaning 'little road'. This is a rough track. We follow it and a man directs us to a gate. There is a circular stone wall with a couple of stone steps down to the shallow water in the bottom of the well, then a channel of water running into a second stone cavity and out into a narrow stream, surrounded by boggy ground. It is called *Tobar Iosa*, which means Well of Jesus, but it actually goes back to pre-Christian days. We are the only people here, and it feels magical to be at this secret forgotten place.

Near the well is a rough stone altar, on which stand three pieces of stone. On the centre one which is over 1200 years old is a carving of a small cross in a circle. This altar was used as a mass rock 300 years ago when, due to the Penal Laws, it was difficult and dangerous to hold a Catholic mass. Services had no regular schedules. When the next one would be was communicated by word of mouth.

Beside the well is a holly tree. To the Celts holly represented balance and ensured the rebirth of the year. The holly's wood is whiter than any other wood and symbolises a light within, despite a dark outer world.

Like at St Brigid's Well, dozens of ribbons and pieces of material have been tied to the tree. These token pieces of clothing are known as 'clooties'. I really love the symbolism of this—the prayers, wishes and worries of life being given up to the healing powers of the wood and the water as the clooties turn to rags in the wind and rain.

One of my small efforts to help the environment is to use handkerchiefs rather than tissues. When my father died I inherited his drawer of large red spotty handkerchiefs. So with the new nail scissors I cut up one of these and Jeremy and I both attach a piece to the tree. Tying the strip of the handkerchief to the tree I smile at the thought of how my father always used to carry a small box of snuff and take a pinch if he came in contact anyone with a cold, while my mother lambasted him for what she regarded as a ridiculous habit. Then I wish for a successful journey along the rest of St Declan's Way.

At that moment an old man wearing a tweed cap and jacket appears with his dog, and remarks what a beautiful spot it is. He adds that the dog loves the place, too. Shortly afterwards I am moving about looking for the best vantage point from which to take a photograph when Jeremy yells, 'Don't step back!' I turn around to see that all around the well are mounds of dog shit. Then I walk over to a bench to sit down. It is permeated with the smell of urine. Suddenly this special sacred spot feels rather sordid, and I am happy when Jeremy suggests that we leave.

We drive back into Cahir and head to the Galtee Inn for a drink and some food. As we talk he tells me about his family, and the exotic tastes of his six-year-old son, who recently requested moules marinières for his birthday dinner.

Afterwards I get a lift back to Lisakyle from the manager of the Galtee Inn, John, who tells me he is running someone else out that way. It turns out to be Michael, who for the last half hour, in a drunken haze, has had his head resting on the bar. John tells me to sit in the front and from the back Michael starts mumbling incoherently about going to say the rosary and being in trouble with his mam, interspersed with lots of 'fecks'. Occasionally, he starts to lie down on the black leather seat, at which point John roars at him not to go to sleep, and he drags himself up again.

John drops Michael off, and then leaves me at Lisakyle. The hostel is in complete darkness. Maurice has told me to lock the door, as I am the only person staying here this evening. I turn the key in the lock and then discover that this was probably a rather superfluous gesture as half the downstairs windows do not even close.

I sit at the table in the sitting room writing my journal. Then I realise that the two pieces of homemade soda bread which the lovely Lithuanian lady at the Galtee Inn had put in plastic wrap for me must have fallen out of my bag when I got out of the car. I have a spasmodic night's sleep, as my mind debates whether, given the loss of the soda bread, I should walk back into Cahir first thing in the morning for supplies or if I'll make it to Ardfinnan tomorrow on short rations. Admittedly I also feel a bit nervous about being in this unfamiliar house alone, so have half an ear out for strange sounds, and drift in and out of sleep listening to the rain.

13

Backtracking

Daylight is streaming through the window when I finally open my eyes. I go downstairs and open the front door. It's overcast and the air is damp. I walk across to the far side of the road where John dropped me off yesterday, and to my delight find the two pieces of soda bread still tightly wrapped in their plastic. The gravel drive is wet from last night's downpour and the plastic wrap is splattered with raindrops. But inside the bread is completely dry, so I take it back indoors and toast it for breakfast.

Lisakyle is south of Cahir and actually on St Declan's Way, but because I got a lift into Cahir with the French couple yesterday morning and back last night with John, I have not walked the section of the Way between the Swiss Cottage and here. So I head up the road planning to take, what on the map, looks like a pretty riverside walk back again.

In the car park at the Swiss Cottage I meet three middle-aged women. I ask them if they know this river walk. One says that the path has been churned up by horses and is impassable, but as she's wearing a tailored coat and skirt and high-heeled shoes I decide that she probably doesn't walk much, so I'll follow it anyway.

The path is a grass track along the banks of the River Suir. As I watch the water of the wide river rolling on its way, it reminds me of my favourite walk on the inches of the mighty Blackwater River below the castle at Lismore. I take a deep breath of morning air and am so glad that I wasn't put off by the woman in the car park.

Five minutes later my joy evaporates. The path turns up into the woodlands and I face a large pool of mud. There's no way around it, so I step forward and watch with a sinking heart as my new black suede boots disappear into the slop. They emerge a hideous shade of brown. Assuming I'm through the worst of it I keep going. From then on the path is quagmire after quagmire of dark sticky mud heavily studded with hoof marks. With every step more rich earth sticks to my boots and they get heavier and heavier.

According to the map the path follows the river then veers left to meet the road. After walking up through the woodlands for ten minutes I assume I must be nearly at the road, so at the top of a hill I continue following the track round to the left rather than taking a narrower path to the right. Around every bend I think I'll come out onto the road, but the path goes on and on, until eventually I arrive back at the Swiss Cottage, having just done a large circle.

What I thought would be a pleasant mile-and-a-half morning stroll has been twice that distance and most of it through thick mud, a disheartening start to the day. But I am cheered up almost immediately by finding a bank of wild raspberries. The deep pinky-purple berries are perfectly ripe, so I cram them into my mouth, savouring their exquisitely delicious flavour. Is this my prize, I wonder? The reward for walking in a large muddy circle in order to learn to let go of expectations and heed the wise warnings of others.

I don't get back to the hostel until after half past ten, which is the time I'm meant to be out. However, as there's no sign of Maurice I decide to clean my boots before leaving. I find a sponge behind a pot of geraniums near the front door, and have almost finished scrubbing the mud off one boot, when Maurice appears saying I must leave immediately. He's in a hurry and needs to lock up. So I dump all my belongings outside the front door, and once he has driven off I find a rainwater butt in the yard. I finish cleaning my boots there while a couple of inquisitive farm cats peer at me from behind a stack of planks in an open shed.

Before I leave I take a final look at the hostel. The yard is swept and clean, and the garden at the front of the old farm house is very well kept. There are hanging baskets of flowers either side of the freshly painted front door and pots of brightly coloured geraniums along the front of the house. Like so many things on this journey, nothing is quite how it appears. As I head out onto the road, I almost wonder if I've imagined its grubby interior.

From here St Declan's Way follows the main road to Ardfinnan for a bit over a mile before it turns off onto a smaller road. Cars drive fast along this stretch, so I am constantly taking to the ditch. It seems to take a long time to reach the turning and I begin to wonder whether I'm actually walking an Irish mile, which is in fact the equivalent of a mile and a quarter. Seeing two men working in a driveway, I stop to ask directions. As we're talking a car pulls in. It's Jeremy, looking very business like this morning in a shirt and tie. He's just had a meeting in Ardfinnan and is now on his way to Dublin airport. He gives me a map of Ardfinnan, so I'll be able to find my way around when I get there, then drives off.

Eventually, I reach the turn-off. The back road is quiet and having walked for an hour and a half I sit beside a farm gate and eat lunch. Beads of water from last night's rain glisten like gaudy baubles on top of the long thick blades of grass. I watch a black spider moving from one blade to another. The more I walk the more I'm starting to take in tiny details in the world around me. It's a luxury that there's rarely time for in my normal busy life. Most days my mind is racing, thinking about all the people I need to catch up with and the endless checklist for work. But now nothing is pressing in on me. Something else is happening as well. I'm becoming aware of the little synchronicities—like bumping into Jeremy again and meeting Charles Hazell in Cashel—which add something magical to my days. Also, I'm starting to read the signposts around me in nature. I smile to myself when I start walking again and immediately see a pied wagtail, that bird of good luck, perched on a pile of wood.

From my resting place the road heads up onto the ridge of a hill. To the south across the valley I see for the first time the distinctive contour of the Knockmealdown Mountains.

A surge of excitement runs through me when I see these familiar rounded mountains which divide Tipperary and Waterford. Whenever I came back from Dublin I always knew when they came into sight that I was nearly home. Looking up the Blackwater River from the old ferry wharf at Camphire they always looked purple in the evening light. On the road to Cappoquin I loved seeing them rolling up and down in the distance, with the Knockmealdown itself in the middle—bigger and higher, like a great mother to the rest of the range. Though I no longer live in Ireland, when I see these mountains I feel part of them. But now a thought crosses my mind like a dark shadow. I wonder if I'll always feel this delight at seeing them, or if one day I'll just view them dispassionately, like a house I used to live in but no longer have any connection with. The home that they represent is this land I know so well, but also the home created by my parents which is now gone. With my father's death my mother has given up on life, too. She used to be so social and flamboyant—she loved having people to stay, holding dances and throwing dinner parties—but now she has fallen into a black abyss of depression and can barely look after herself.

I am so absorbed in my thoughts I miss the turning to Ardfinnan. I reach a crossroads and realise I'm back on the main road. Beginning to feel tired and footsore again I'm angry with myself for not concentrating.

A man in a four-wheel drive stops so I ask him directions. Initially, he's adamant that if I want to go to Ardfinnan I must take the busy main road. He admits, though, that he would not want to walk down the main road to Ardfinnan because there are too many cars. Then he adds that he would not want to take the side road I'm looking for either, though he doesn't explain why. Finally he gives me some vague directions back the way I have just come. It's only in Ireland that you get such a convoluted response, and still end up none the wiser. I think I was asking for reassurance more than anything else. I wanted to be told just to go back a couple of hundred yards and I couldn't miss it. But instead all I got was confusion.

I retrace my steps and find the turning onto a narrow unmarked road. I walk down the hill towards Ardfinnan, then, as I pass a yard full of chickens, the road goes up again. I'm on the outskirts the village now and on top of a hill is a small stone Church of Ireland. It is built on the original site of St Finian's monastery. St Finian was known as Finian the Leper because people from all over Ireland came to him to be healed, especially of skin diseases, and eventually he contracted leprosy.

I push open the old gate into the churchyard. The grass is so high the gravestones are barely visible and I wonder why it's been so neglected. I walk around the small church looking for an open door, but it's firmly locked up. Having been baptised into the Church of Ireland, a part of me still has a connection to it, even though I've found solace and inspiration from many other sources beyond it. My relationship with the church today is like one with an old friend I've lost touch with. The initial spark which brought us together is gone, but a fondness and sense of gratitude for everything they gave me remains. I stand at the door and long to be able to spend a quiet moment inside.

I lean my backpack up against the back of the building and set off up the road to find a large fairy rath which is supposedly not far away, and look around the village.

I pass the castle built by Prince John, which still stands on the hill overlooking the river. At first glance it looks like a ruin, with ivy growing over the tops of the walls, but then I notice the windows are in good repair. I later learn that an old lady lives here alone and apparently she's a recluse. Ardfinnan, with its population of about 1000 people, has grown up either side of the River Suir. For centuries the fordability of the river made Ardfinnan a place of strategic importance, but it also made it vulnerable to attack, such as when the marauding Normans burnt down St Finian's monastery 800 years ago. I cross over the fourteen-arched stone bridge to the other side of the village. I pass the school, and further down the main street are the catholic church, the post office, a few pubs and some shops. After admiring a gaggle of geese on the village green I walk back over the bridge and go in search of the rath.

I can't find it, there is no one around, and the only place to ask is a motorbike repair shop. Two men in the driveway are studying a very powerful-looking Yamaha and completely ignore me as I approach, but the man behind the counter inside gives me directions. He explains the rath's just above a sandpit further up the road, although doesn't mention the high electronic gate across the entrance to it. The fairies are proving elusive to say the least. There are no more raths along the next section of St Declan's Way and I'm despondent about my chances of ever getting the opportunity to have a close look at one of these mysterious places.

Footsore and frustrated I plod back towards the church, but I am stopped in my tracks at a green where two roads meet. A small white feather flutters in the slight breeze above a stone memorial. As I approach I see the memorial is dedicated to all those who fell victim to the potato famine of the mid-nineteenth century, that caused hundreds of thousands of deaths and over a million people to leave their home country forever.

14

Castle Grace

B ack at the church I find an elderly man with a loud electric trimmer slashing the long grass. Apparently the church is now being used as a scout hall. I also discover Castle Grace, where I'm staying the night with old friends Nicholas and Barbara Grubb, is at least 4 miles away. Despite my initial intention to walk I decide to ring Barbara and see if she'd mind coming to collect me. Twenty minutes later she pulls up at the petrol station and grocery store just before the stone bridge. She gives me a kiss on the cheek and greets me as if we only saw each other a couple of days ago.

I met Nicholas and Barbara my first Christmas at Lismore. Barbara's parents, James and Emily Villiers-Stuart, invited our family to dinner on Christmas Day. I was so touched that these people we had barely met included us in their family Christmas, and they have been great friends ever since.

Driving along the narrow country road we pass the enormous empty five-storey mill, then immediately turn up the sweeping gravel drive to the large eight-bedroom house built by the Grubb family nearly 200 years ago. On the lawn are a gaggle of geese that Barbara is fattening up for Christmas. We are met by a pack of enthusiastic labradors, Jack Russells and Cairn terriers. Nicholas appears and, as the sun is currently shining, we take deckchairs out onto the croquet lawn and have tea in the garden. Beyond the lawn is the apple orchard and to the south the Sugarloaf Mountain can be clearly seen.

Nicholas and Barbara are in constant motion. In the early 1970s Nicholas, with a handful of other people, introduced Limousin cattle to Ireland and for the next 30 years he and Barbara kept more than 100 head of these pedigree French cattle. Barbara was also secretary of the Irish Limousin Cattle Society for many years. Nicholas, now in his late 50s, is very tall and thin and extremely energetic and also eccentric. He constantly comes up with innovative ideas. He single-handedly harvests Castle Grace's 20 acres of cider apples every year.

Also tall and thin, and very pretty, Barbara is equally busy and usually followed by the pack of dogs. This afternoon she is preparing for the next round of guests staying in the Mill and Dower Houses, which she lets out on a weekly basis. She rushes into her office to check an email and sits at her desk which is covered in precariously high piles of papers.

I follow the two Jack Russells into the wood-panelled sitting room. One of the Cairns is sitting on a Persian rug licking its paw, and is promptly joined by the golden labrador, Grouse. On the table is a copy of the *Irish Farmers Journal*, a sewing basket, and a pile of *The Field* magazines. On the radiator sits a brown leather-bound book entitled *Daniel's Rural*

Sports. I open it to see a signature and the date 1808 written on the inside cover. Then I notice a black leather-bound bible on a wooden chest under the window. It was printed by Oxford University Press in 1804 and has the name 'Margaret Grubb, 1854' written on the first page. Touchingly, there's a small piece of unfinished tapestry of a cross sticking out of the righthand corner.

The Grubbs first settled in this part of Ireland more than 300 years ago. The family were originally Quakers, but Nicholas's great-grandfather was expelled from the order for going to a dance. Although there were few Quakers in the area their impact was huge. They built all the mills and built and lived in nearly all the big houses. They also monopolised the grain trade at the time of its greatest prosperity.

After tea I walk down past the still headstream of the river surrounded by tall green reeds to have a closer look at the mill. This huge edifice looks like something out of a Charles Dickens novel. Opening a large corrugated iron sliding door I let myself in and wander through the vast empty building, avoiding the few rotting floorboards and broken steps. Several floors up are piles of wooden crates, and round wicker baskets and their lids, which were used for sending produce from here to London's fruit and vegetable market at Covent Garden.

At the start of the Second World War Nicholas's grandfather established an enterprise at the mill, gathering and processing rural Irish products. Sloes were collected to make sloe gin, and crab apples were picked for jelly. Thousands of tonnes of blackberries were also gathered by hundreds of children across southern Ireland. They were paid half a crown for each stone of fruit, a significant addition to many families' budgets. When the blackberries arrived at Castle Grace they were cooked, preserved, put in wooden barrels and sent to Robertsons of Bristol for their world-famous jam.

Nicholas remembers elderberries being collected, too. Their juice was sent in gallon tins to New York where an enterprising Mr Hartog, in the religious wine trade, used the juice to colour white Portuguese port. White port was far cheaper than the red variety and once the elderberry concentrate was added, the clerics knew no difference.

At one stage 60 people worked at the mill. Most were involved in the processing of poultry. The birds were killed, plucked, cleaned and immediately transported to Cahir in time for the overnight train then ferry to London. Mrs Lonergan from Clogheen became a bit of a legend. She was known as the Queen of the Pluckers and did not miss a shift even when she had a baby. After finishing the 4 a.m. shift, she gave birth to a fine strong boy, and returned back to work that night.

Today, Nicholas is using the same water force that his family used to drive the mill to create hydro-electricity. It provides all the power for the main house and the three houses they let out, and energy is also fed back into the grid.

Barbara and I walk down to the walled garden. It is formally laid out with a sundial in the middle and four 200-year-old Irish yew trees. Along the walls are magnolias and climbing roses. A couple of the walls are part of the original Castle Grace, the now ruined Norman castle. A large wisteria with its delicate lilac flowers grows beside one of the old castle towers.

A doorway in one wall leads through to the large walled vegetable garden below. Growing here are plum trees, raspberry, and black and white currant bushes, as well as lettuces and runner beans. A few chickens peer at us from a pen at the far end. While Barbara digs up some potatoes I walk into the field behind the walled garden to look at the outside of the crumbling ivy-covered castle. It was built by Raymond Le Gros, the brother-in-law of the powerful Norman warlord Strongbow. In the 1970s the castle featured in the Stanley Kubrick film, *Barry Lyndon*, which, Barbara adds, netted a nice bit of income that helped renovate the house.

The Normans' presence in Ireland came about due to a power struggle between two Irish kings over control of Dublin, which even 850 years ago was already recognised as the power-base for the control of the whole of Ireland. When Rory O'Connor, the king of Connaught, ousted Dermot MacMurrough, the king of Leinster, from Dublin and had himself inaugurated as high-king, MacMurrough appealed to King Henry II of England for help.

As Henry II was unable to go to Ireland himself at this time, he accepted homage and a pledge of loyalty from Dermot MacMurrough, and authorised his subjects to go instead. So King Dermot approached the Earl of Pembroke, known as Strongbow, for help and offered him his daughter Aoife in marriage and the whole province of Leinster after his death. The other Norman barons he recruited included Maurice FitzGerald and Robert FitzStephen, both sons of the Welsh princess Nesta, and he offered them County Wexford for their services.

Interestingly Barbara's family were originally FitzGeralds and can trace their origins back to the Norman baron Maurice FitzGerald, who came to Ireland with Strongbow in the twelfth century. When her father James Villiers-Stuart died in 2004 Barbara inherited Dromana, the family home, which was also originally a Norman stronghold. It is built high up on a cliff above the Blackwater River south of Lismore.

As we walk back to the house Barbara looks at her watch and suddenly realises we're going to be late for the dinner party we have been invited to in Lismore tonight. I dash upstairs to put on my rather crumpled skirt and top. Nicholas drives at high speed along the mountain road, avoiding the sheep stretched out on the warm bitumen.

Our host, Peter Raven, lives at Ballyinn, a pretty house on the opposite side of the Blackwater River from the castle. As it's a sunny evening we have drinks in the beautiful garden which slopes down to the bank of the river. There are ten of us for dinner. I sit next to a scientist called Moira Gallagher who, with her long blonde hair, looks exactly like an Irish queen. Due to the increase in the price of oil, there is a lot of talk about hydro-electricity as several guests debate whether the river or stream running through their land could be utilised for power.

As I get into bed that evening I think of the dinner parties my mother used to have at Lismore Castle. Marabella loved entertaining and once or twice a week she would hold a dinner party and there would be eight or ten people around the long mahogany dining room table. She had a flair for whipping up a delicious three-course meal. Fresh vegetables came from the castle garden and in summer we ate salmon and sea trout from the Blackwater River. Then we would adjourn to the drawing room for coffee and liqueurs and my father in his green velvet smoking jacket would seat himself at the grand piano with a glass of scotch and a Turkish cigarette and play jazz.

I think of the time and effort Peter put into the evening tonight, organising the wine and the delicious food, and deciding who should sit next to who at the table. Everyone was so exuberant as they chatted and ate and I felt very honoured to be there.

15

Lost on the mountain

I t's day five. I'm lying in bed savouring that delectable moment of complete comfort on waking and wish it would last forever. Then I see a long thin worm wiggling across the crisp white sheet. I make a half-hearted attempt to catch it and fail, and by the time I get out of bed and search properly it has disappeared. Then I start to worry that I might be the carrier of the worm. This is followed by the realisation that I should confess its presence and my possible responsibility for it to Barbara. Fortunately, she's not concerned that her spare bed is now home to a worm.

Susie Wingfield is walking with me over the mountain today. When I was eighteen and first moved to Dublin to go to drama school, Susie and her husband, Philip, who used to work for the Bank of Ireland, very kindly let me stay with them and their three children for the first couple of months. We have been friends ever since. Philip and Susie now live at Salterbridge near Cappoquin on the southern side of the

Knockmealdowns. Barbara has invited Susie and Philip to breakfast. They arrive at nine o'clock, saying the visibility is so bad up the mountain that driving here they were unable to see more than a few yards in front of them. Given these adverse conditions, Barbara lends us a map of the local area and also a compass so we don't get lost.

Although the mountains are not high, it's easy to lose your way in bad weather. This is what happened to Lismore's famous travel writer, Dervla Murphy, when she was a child. She had cycled up from Lismore and decided to climb to the top of Knockmealdown, which is small as mountains go, just under 3000 feet. The weather changed, clouds formed then dusk fell. Disorientated and having wandered for hours, Dervla eventually came across an unoccupied animal shelter, built of stone with a turf roof, where she spent the night.

Philip drives us to Ardfinnan, so that we can rejoin St Declan's Way from the stone bridge where Barbara picked me up yesterday. Today Susie and I are walking up over Bottleneck Pass to Castle Doddard, which is on the County Waterford side of the Knockmealdowns. Because Philip will be picking up Susie from Castle Doddard later in the day, he offers to transport my backpack so I don't have to carry it.

Susie and I follow a path in between some houses in the village and out onto the old road, passing a ruined stone building which was a fever hospital during the famine. More people died of cholera and typhoid during the famine than they did of starvation. Tragically people flocked to the over-crowded workhouses to get food, and it was in these places that the diseases abounded.

Boundless energy makes Susie one of life's special people. She helped set up the Cystic Fibrosis Research Trust in Ireland. Cystic fibrosis is particularly prevalent in Ireland. Ironically it's the same gene that carries this debilitating disease which gives immunity to cholera and typhoid. This is thought be to be the reason why such a high percentage of people in Ireland are carriers of the gene, because their ancestors survived the famine.

Ten minutes later we stop at the ruins of Lady's Abbey, which 600 years ago was a Carmelite friary. A limestone tower with its arched entrance still stands, and in a wall beyond it is a beautiful Celtic-style arched window. Like at the Rock of Cashel gravestones are dotted around the ruined building.

Susie is an excellent walking companion. She has a great knowledge of wild flowers. She points out the snowberry with its white puffballs, and the tiny white eyebright with its sunny yellow centres. As its name suggests this plant was used in traditional medicine for soothing sore eyes.

St Declan's Way, or the Way of Patrick's Cow, as this part of the way is known, becomes a boreen. Having pushed our way through a bramble hedge to avoid a deep muddy puddle, we reach a footbridge over the River Tar. Here St Declan's Way joins the walking track called the Tipperary Heritage Way and there are numerous small wooden signposts pointing us in the right direction.

We have been steadily walking uphill and are now at the foot of the Knockmealdowns. We pass rowans with their bright blazing red berries hanging in clusters. These elegant, slender trees are also known as mountain ash, or quickbeam, and are said to symbolise action and energy. The rowan's Irish name is *caorthann*, which comes from the word *caor* meaning both a berry and a blazing flame. In the ancient Irish Ogham alphabet, each letter is named after a different tree and the rowan is associated with the letter *luis*, which means flame. As rowan berries bear the sign of a pentagon, it is considered a very protective tree, often used for warding off enchantments. Its red berries are also thought to imbue the tree with magical powers.

The track climbs through a forest. A sign points to the right, but, according to the map, St Declan's Way is left so we take the left turning. As we climb higher the weather fluctuates between pockets of sunshine and the soft misty rain that I'm so fond of. Lilac-coloured ling heather and the fuchsia-pink bell heather cover the banks. Tightly knit spiders' webs are suspended from the spiky gorse, catching fine droplets of rain which glisten like jewels in the sunlight. The finely woven webs look like cradles for baby fairies, Susie remarks, as we stop to admire these exquisite natural creations, and imagine the tiny otherworldly beings lying nestled in the prickly gorse for safety.

A little further on the Tipperary Heritage Way turns to the right and crosses a bridge, while St Declan's Way continues straight ahead. Initially, we follow the steep track up the mountain, but when I look at the map I suspect we should be heading further west, so we turn back and take another track. As we climb higher we cross little streams buffered by cushions of sphagnum and bright green Catherine moss. A wide stream bubbles over the rocks as it cascades down the mountain. On its banks grow ferns and foxgloves.

Tall majestic plants with striking purple flowers, foxgloves are believed to be fairy plants. In some regions of Ireland it is said that the foxglove bends its head as a sign of respect if a fairy host is passing by. It was considered the king of Irish herbs and its juice was used to cure those wasting away due to fairy influence. Foxglove tea was also drunk for colds, sore throats and fevers, while foxglove salve was used to treat wounds, burns, swellings and other skin complaints. But, although the traditional herbalists used them successfully for a broad range of ailments, and they are the source of digitalis, which is used today by the pharmaceutical industry to treat heart conditions, foxgloves are extremely toxic and all parts of the plant are actually poisonous.

After about a mile and a half we realise the track we are following is going around the mountain rather than over it. We've been enjoying the walk so much we're not particularly concerned. We sit in the rain, eating the delicious salami sandwiches Barbara has made for us, before again retracing our steps back to where we deviated from the signposts. We turn back onto the track heading up the mountain which we originally took hours earlier. I keep looking at the map. None of the markings make sense, but at least we are walking uphill.

Then the stillness is broken by Susie's mobile. It's Philip. He wants to know where we are. Susie tells him optimistically that we have found the right path and are nearly over the mountain.

We emerge out of the woodland and into the heather. Through the mist I can just make out a cairn a couple of hundred yards up ahead. Moments later it disappears in a mass of white cloud. There's no sign of a path through the heather, so I get the compass out. We head south hoping we'll reach Bottleneck Pass, which is the county boundary between Tipperary and Waterford. From there if we head straight down the other side of the mountain we should be at Castle Doddard.

About ten minutes later Susie stoops down and picks a handful of hurts. I savour these small juicy bilberries and only later discover it is considered very bad luck to eat them after the Irish harvest festival *Lúghnasa*, which was nearly a month ago. Barely have I swallowed the berries, when she suggests we turn back. It's quarter to five. Time is getting on. We need to keep moving. I desperately want to get over the pass, but when I look at her, up to her knees in heather with the rain swirling around her, and the mountain in a white blanket of mist, I reluctantly agree. I know it is easy to get disorientated up here, especially in these conditions.

We turn round to find the woodlands are now engulfed in cloud and totally invisible. We head downhill and eventually reach the barbed wire fence enclosing the forestry. Susie rings Philip and asks him to meet us on the road out of Ardfinnan. I feel utterly despondent. We have spent the entire day looking for the right way and not found it. I still have no idea of how to get across the mountain, so it's not as if I can head off alone tomorrow knowing where to go. I keep running round and round in my mind where we might have gone wrong, but don't find an answer.

As much as I hate giving up and the thought of an incomplete journey, I borrow Susie's mobile and ring Barbara to explain the predicament and ask if I can stay another night. Then, because Susie and I are both tired, we wander off in the wrong direction, adding another mile and a half to our walk before we finally reach where Philip is waiting for us in the car.

It's nearly seven o'clock when, in soaking wet boots and with a new blister, I arrive back at Castle Grace. Nicholas returns at the same time after a day of fighting the wild purple-flowering *Rhododendron ponticum* with a Russian at Dromana. It sounds like a series of near-death experiences as he wrestled with the chainsaw and the rhododendron branches sprang back at him.

While Nicholas disappears with my boots to dry them under an industrial dryer of some sort, I take the black bucket from the back door, head to the vegetable garden and dig up some pink-skinned potatoes, called British queens, which Barbara roasts in the oven for supper. Then she suggests I have a bath.

Lying fully immersed in the huge green enamelled bathtub at the back of the house, I'm in a state of bliss. Despite the major setback it has been another wonderful day. It was magical up on the mountain in the mist.

16

Bay Lough and Petticoat Loose

Unlike yesterday it is sunny this morning, and Sugarloaf, the small conical mountain this end of the Knockmealdown range, can be seen clearly from Castle Grace. Despite talking to Nicholas last night, I still don't have a clear idea of the route St Declan's Way takes over the mountain, so decide to walk straight up the mountain from Castle Grace via the Vee instead. The Vee is the pass through which the road runs. I'm consoled by the fact that it's the suggested route for St Declan pilgrims if the weather is bad.

Barbara gives me directions which take me part of the way through woodlands rather than along the road. Because she is driving over the mountain to Dromana later in the day, she offers to leave my backpack beside the statue of the virgin at the top, so I don't have to carry it up.

With no backpack to burden me, a carefully plastered toe and dry boots it is the perfect day. I feel all is well with the world again as I leave Castle Grace, past the mill along the narrow road. On the banks grow pink-flowering woundwort, the leaves of which were used for dressing wounds. Beside it grows the thistle-like knapweed and spearmint with its small lilac flowers. Rising up ahead of me is Sugarloaf Hill and to the west are the gentle sloping Galtee Mountains. It's a delight walking in a place that's so familiar to me and to have time to enjoy it. I listen to the gurgling of a mountain stream hidden in the undergrowth beside the road and watch a bumblebee hovering above a single stem of centaury with its pink pointy-stemmed petals. The Irish name for centaury is *Dréimire Mhuire*, meaning Mary's ladder. This pretty plant growing here on a small grass knoll is said to be the ladder the Virgin Mary used to ascend to heaven.

As the road climbs purple-headed scabious and clusters of eyebright give way to bell and ling heather and yellow flowering gorse. Following Barbara's instructions I turn off the road into Kilballyboy Wood and cross over the main road from Clogheen, the village below. Hopping over the stone wall, I find myself in a stand of Scots pines. A couple of tyre tracks lead up the hill to what looks like a forestry track ahead. This is the route Barbara told me to take.

Almost instantly the track becomes a narrow path along a bed of soft moss. Either side of it the trunks of the trees and their low branches are coated in a thin layer of bright green moss, too. The path gets narrower and I feel as if I am walking into some enchanted place. Stooping lower to pass under the ever-tightening crisscross of velvety emerald-covered limbs, I realise this mossy path is running along the side of the mountain not up it. In a gloomy moment I wonder if I am destined to remain trapped in Tipperary forever.

I turn back into the more open woodland and beside two bright yellow tormantil flowers is a path upwards. It takes me to a wide track which heads up the mountain. A fritillary with its delicate gold and brown wings flutters just ahead of me as Sugarloaf Hill again comes into view through a clearing in the trees. I know now I'm on the right path. A young couple with a dog stride up behind me. They are also going to the Vee, so we walk up together.

Just below the Vee we reach the dark waters of Bay Lough. The man tells me his father used to swim here as a child. He says he's heard the lough is bottomless and I've been told a similar story. Apparently the men from Clogheen came up one day to measure the depth of Bay Lough. But when they looked at the village below them they saw their houses on fire, so they ran back down the mountain as fast as they could. They got home and discovered it was just an illusion: their houses weren't on fire at all. The following day they walked back up to Bay Lough, and again they saw their houses burning. Again they ran back down the mountain only to find their homes were fine. When this happened a third time they realised they were not meant to know the depth of the lough.

Another legend says that St Patrick gathered up all the monsters in Ireland and put them in Bay Lough. He told them to stay there and that he would be back tomorrow, but he never came back, so they are there still.

These tales certainly capture the mood of the lake. It's a dark and eerie place. There's something about it that keeps you on edge. I have swum in Bay Lough a couple of times, but even though I'm a confident swimmer, I never dared to swim across the middle. I was told if I did I could be pulled down into the depths by Petticoat Loose.

Petticoat Loose was a red-haired woman who came from around Colligan, near Dungarvan, and was fond of dancing. One day her petticoat came undone while she was dancing in a pub and that's how she got her nickname.

Our family friend Kieran Heffernan, who is also a local historian, told me that her real name was Brigit and she was a strong hard-headed farmer, who used to wrestle and fight the local men. It's said that once she killed a cow with one blow of her fist. She fell out with the church, and apparently that was her downfall.

In the 1820s and 1830s Petticoat Loose used to drink in Quills Pub while mass was being held at the church. One Sunday a travelling farmhand from the west of Ireland came to the pub looking for the money she owed him. She took his spade off him and swung it at his neck, killing him. Then she threatened everyone at the pub with the same fate if they said anything. So the pub's patrons denied that they saw anything, and Petticoat Loose wasn't prosecuted because there were no witnesses. After her death, though, some of them came forward and admitted she murdered the farmhand.

It is said that Petticoat Loose came back to haunt people because she had committed murder and died without going to confession and getting absolution. She would write a sign on the door of a home with butter, bringing the occupants nothing but bad luck. People would be driving cattle to a fair in the very early morning, when it was still dark, and meet her ghost on the road. She would put a hex on the cattle and scatter them or drive them wild. For some unknown reason, though, she would never interfere with anyone by the name of John.

Kieran's grandfather met Petticoat Loose on the road from Tallow once, and was absolutely terrified. His neighbour Pat O'Keeffe was coming home from the mill in Tallow with a load of freshly ground oats, when Petticoat Loose jumped up on his cart. She flogged the horse which took off at a great pace. Pat O'Keeffe was hanging on for dear life, screamed at her to stop, but she wouldn't. She kept beating the horse until they reached his house. Then she disappeared and the exhausted horse dropped dead.

Finally, about 80 years after she died, the local people had had enough of her antics and sent for a priest who was experienced in exorcisms. Because she was a very strong spirit, he was not able to exorcise her completely. Instead he banished her to Bay Lough and gave her something to do that took up her time, so she would not disturb people. Some people say she has to make the shapes of horses' collars with stones. Others say he gave her the task of emptying the lough with a bottomless saucepan.

Whether or not Petticoat Loose resides in the lough, I don't even contemplate a swim today. The air has a cold twinge to it and, although the sun was shining brightly a moment ago, now there is a black cloud overhead, and this dark basin of water looks more ominous than ever.

As I sit on a limestone rock overlooking the lough, a pale yellow crab spider negotiates the gorse beside me. Every so often there's a loud plop as a fish jumps out of the water. A swallow skims past me. Then I hear someone calling my name. A golden labrador appears beside me, and just as I realise it is Grouse, Barbara strides up with the Jack Russells at her heels. She was worried that I might have got lost and has come looking for me. Realising that I have not established a great reputation for finding my way, I don't mention the mossy detour.

Nicholas, she tells me, has both measured the depth of the lough and also swam across it. The reason for the drownings, he reckons, are not because of Petticoat Loose dragging swimmers down into the depths, but the extreme cold of the water just below the surface. When a person swims out to the middle of the lough and stops to wave at friends and family on the shore, the lower part of their body is upright in the water, and can't cope with the ferocious cold beneath the surface and so they drown. Either way I still don't feel like a dip today.

As we walk with the dogs around the lough and up towards the road, Barbara tells me that, although it is accessible to the public, the lough is actually on Grubb land. Also, she adds, it is a favoured spot for people to commit suicide by gassing themselves in their cars, and for that reason she has been tempted at times to put up a sign saying, 'No suicides'. Then she confides that her great-great-aunt Pauline's sweetheart was probably the first person to commit suicide here. He was an engineer and was building the railway line at Cappoquin when Pauline and he met and fell in love. But Pauline's father refused him her hand in marriage. He didn't like the young man's prospects, and thought he didn't come from a good enough family for his daughter. So Pauline's suitor killed himself at Bay Lough. Ironically, had he lived he would have come into a substantial inheritance and a title, which in Pauline's father's eyes would have made him most eligible for his daughter.

Barbara leads me up the track from the lough to the Vee where she has parked her car. She's concerned that someone might have stolen my backpack from where she left it beside the statue of the virgin even though she put a note on it. Given the hideous heaviness of it, I doubt anyone would dream of making off with it and sure enough it's still tucked behind the statue just where she left it.

Barbara quips, as she zooms off in the car with the dogs, that unlike the Virgin at nearby Mount Melleray, this statue doesn't move.

I look at the white statue of Our Lady on top of a stone plinth. In front of her has been placed a small painted rock on which is written: 'Mother, I trust in you'.

Beside the statue is an arched stone building, with an iron gate across the front and a single window at the rear of it, which used to be where the change horses were held for the Waterford–Dublin coach. More recently a stone altar has been built inside for the services held up here. Standing at the top of the Vee I can see the plains of Tipperary stretching for miles below. I feel an enormous sense of achievement to have finally made it up the mountain and into County Waterford.

Rather than walk along the road, which being a Sunday is busy today, I follow a path through the heather slightly to the west of it and then alongside a plantation of Norway spruce. When it starts to head west I decide to follow a forest track which runs more or less parallel with the road, then take another one down to a ford across the Owenashad. The Owenashad, which means 'river of jewels' in Irish, runs down to Lismore where just beyond the castle it joins the mighty Blackwater. Kieran Heffernan told me that the Owenashad got the name because one of the former dukes of Devonshire introduced the cultivation of freshwater pearls in this little river. The industry did not thrive as the water was too cold, but at least the duchess got a gold brooch made from a particularly fine pearl from the river.

As I look at the crystal-clear water gushing over the large stones, it seems faster and deeper than I remember it. I used to come up here with my cousins and paddle. Perhaps the river is deeper because of all the rain this summer. I take off my boots and pick my way gingerly across to the other side, where there's a track leading back to the road.

It is about half past five by the time I rejoin the road from the Vee. I'm alone except for some mountain sheep grazing among a couple of derelict stone cottages. There are not many cars now, but the ditches are festooned with empty beer cans, plastic bottles and biscuit packets. With yellow-flowering gorse growing on the banks and the mountain land a blaze of purple heather, it is incredibly beautiful along this road. The rubbish makes me wonder if our disposable society gives no thought to beauty, or perhaps no thought to how easily we can destroy it.

17

Pepperpots and fairy apparel

An avenue of low hanging trees leads me to Castle Doddard. Looking out onto the purple heather-covered mountain and a lake, Castle Doddard is an enchanting place. My cousins and I used to call it Pepperpots because it is a small castle compared to Lismore. With its round towers and their conical roofs, narrow staircases and maze of rooms full of exquisite drapes and furniture, it seemed to us to be something out of a fairytale.

I open the heavy, wooden front door, climb up the stone staircase and find Pam in the kitchen. Pam Stevenson is now 87 years old. In spite of her age she is still incredibly beautiful and hasn't lost any of her great enthusiasm for life. She is a treasured friend of our family and it's always such a joy to see her. She and her husband, Steve, who is no longer alive, moved to Castle Doddard 40 years ago.

Pam first saw the castle was when she came up for a drive with her brother Rex. 'We saw these three little towers,' she recounts, 'and we walked down the boreen through the brambles and saw this ruin.' Pam fell instantly in love with the place. As they were getting back into the car, they saw a man on a bicycle and asked him if he knew who the towers belonged to. The man took Rex to see the owner. He was sitting on a sack of potatoes, looking at the mountain. When Rex asked if he was selling the ruin, he replied, 'I may and I mayn't.' The next thing Pam saw was Rex shaking hands with the man. He'd bought Pam 12 acres of land and this 350-year-old castle, believed to have been built by the Great Earl of Cork as a hunting lodge, when wolves still roamed the Knockmealdown Mountains.

Pam's life was always extraordinary. She grew up in India where her father was a civil engineer on the railways. When she married Steve, he was in the army and so they lived in numerous places, from India and Egypt, to Libya and Malaysia. Castle Doddard reflects this in the array of exotic items picked up from souks and bazaars. Pam claims her creative flair for design and decoration comes from those days of living in army quarters, and having to create the effect she wanted from whatever materials were at hand. The elegant blue velvet round sofa in the drawing room is actually an old tractor tyre full of padding.

Pam takes me down the narrow stairs in the middle of the castle and shows me my bedroom. Known as 'the blue room', it is on the ground floor and was originally the kitchen. The thick walls are whitewashed, there are wooden beams across the ceiling and three long narrow windows. In the middle of the room is a four-poster bed with a yellow silk canopy, and in the corner a fireplace. Next door is 'the snore room' in which there is another bed. I'm relieved that my husband Stephen isn't here with me tonight as he prods and kicks me whenever I snore and I know, if I even emitted the smallest snort, he would have great delight in banishing me to said snore room.

We have tea in my favourite room of all, the sitting room at the top of the main stairs. This room is a work of art, a conglomeration of objects which sit together perfectly. On a long wooden church seat are a vase of flowers, an Indian picture of an elephant and a wooden candelabra. At one end of the seat is a stone statue of a boy holding a basket and at the other end a statue of a girl. The walls on one side of the room are painted in a muted red wash and stencilled in blue. On the other side the walls are white, contrasting the chaise lounge and a collection of red glass on a table between the two windows.

Pam's daughter Alexandra is staying at the castle with her husband, Nigel, and a friend of theirs, Marianne. Alexandra and Marianne are seated on the old Irish bed with its curved wooden top. Nigel is on the rocking chair, and I'm on a wooden chair covered with an Afghan-looking weave. Pam perches on the little armchair near the Norwegian wood-burning stove, and on the round table are the cheese scones and lemon cake she has made.

Tea slides into drinks and then dinner. Pam tells me that she, too, had heard that St Patrick had gathered all the monsters in Ireland and put them in Bay Lough. Also, she says, when Steve and she first arrived at Castle Doddard, they were informed by their neighbours that Bay Lough was the witch's lake. 'Which witch?' she asked, and was told, 'Petticoat Loose'. Then the neighbour added, 'But there's no fear of her, because wasn't she banished to the black lake, and isn't she there still emptying it with a tailor's thimble?'

Conversation turns to the fairy hat that Meryl Gardner, the friend who first told me about St Declan's Way and lent me her map, found when she was living in the cottage at Castle Doddard twenty years ago. Meryl came across a little grey-coloured fur hat on the driveway. Steve and she photographed it on a foxglove. It was about one-and-a-half inches high and an inch in diameter, Pam says, as she brings out the faded colour photograph of the tiny hat. 'It had a tassel on it,' she explains, 'and a few white hairs. And there were no children in the place at the time so it wasn't a doll's hat.'

Meryl put the hat on a shelf in the kitchen of the cottage then went away for a few days. In her absence Pam was sorting through some papers and found printed on one, 'A leprechaun is not a leprechaun without his hat.' Amused by this she stuck the piece of paper on the front door of the cottage for Meryl to see when she returned. Meryl came home, went to the kitchen and the hat was gone, but neither Steve nor Pam had been into the cottage while she was away and no one else had a key.

Intrigued by the hat, they took the photograph of it to show Olivia Robertson, who is now in her 90s, and lives at Huntington Castle in Clonegal, County Wexford. Olivia is renowned for her psychic ability and her work with other worlds and dimensions. When Meryl and Pam showed her the photograph of the tiny hat, she told them the hat was found by water. This was correct, as it was found on the drive near the lake at Castle Doddard. Also, she said, it belonged to a fairy. So perhaps while Meryl was away that fairy slid under the door of the cottage, or through a crack, and collected his hat.

I stayed at Huntington Castle and met Olivia. When I was living in Dublin I became friends with Olivia's nephew, David, and his wife, Moira. Huntington Castle was built nearly 400 years ago on the site of a medieval Franciscan priory. I was told it was one of the first castles to get electricity. But maybe this initial installation had not been updated since: when I stayed there, although some parts of the castle, like the oak-panelled hallway near the front door, glowed in the electric light, others, including the room where I was sleeping, had none at all.

My room had a four-poster bed in it and, due to the spirit elements also apparently present, was known as the 'four-ghoster'. So I was quite nervous when I blew out my candle and lay there in the dark and the silence, until my robust aptitude for sleep overcame me.

The following morning I came down to breakfast and Olivia, with her long red hair and long purple robe, was sitting at the table eating a boiled egg. Disarmingly, her eyes look in different directions, but she fixed one on me and immediately asked whether I had seen a man carrying his head under his arm last night. When I replied that I had not, she returned to her egg, utterly disinterested in someone so obviously unpsychic.

Olivia's brother, Lawrence Durdin-Robertson, known as Derry, had been a Church of England clergyman before he had the realisation that God was a woman. He proceeded to cut the word 'God' out of all the books in the library, reducing much of the family collection of books, particularly the religious ones, to little more than confetti. Olivia and he founded the Fellowship of Isis, which now has a membership of 27 000 people in more than 100 countries, to support and promote the idea of the divine feminine and awareness of the goddess.

Although at the time I was very disconcerted by Derry and Olivia's eccentricity, I was enchanted by the Temple of Isis, which was in the basement of the castle. In the many alcoves were beautiful wooden sculptures. Elsewhere in the temple were ornamental cats, brightly painted face masks, and Tibetan and Hindu artifacts. I loved the emphasis on the goddess and the Brighid's Well in the middle of the temple. The water from here, Olivia explained, not only had healing properties, but was also meant to develop psychic powers. Despite David telling me earlier that in a recent attempt to remove the Victorian terrace at the front of the castle, Derry had severed the main sewage pipe and the well water should be avoided, I took a large gulp in the hope that it would sharpen my ability to see ghosts.

Looking at Pam's photo of the fairy hat, I am reminded of my only other encounter with fairy apparel. Tom Somerville and I shared a house together in Dublin. We used to spend a considerable amount of time debating one issue or another.

Tom was a barrister, and to my absolute irritation, he always used to confound me with his logic and I had to undergo the humiliation of Tom throwing back his head of curly hair and roaring with victorious laughter.

One weekend Tom invited a group of us to stay at Drushane, his family house in Castletownsend in West Cork. He showed us a very narrow shoe, about 3 inches long, made of what looked like fine leather. He said it had been found 170 years ago by a farm labourer on the Beara Peninsula, who gave it to the local doctor. The doctor passed it to the Somerville family. The first conclusion I jumped to was that it must be a doll's shoe, but Tom pointed out how the instep of the heel of the shoe was worn in a way that would never happen to a shoe worn by a doll. Looking more closely I saw he was right. Except for its size it looked as if it has been worn by a person. Tom told us it was a fairy shoe.

Tom's great-aunt, Dr Edith Somerville, who co-wrote *The Experiences of an Irish RM*, gave the shoe to a group of Harvard University scientists to study while she was on a lecture tour of America. The scientists noted its well-crafted eyelets, even though it had no laces, and said it was made of mouse skin and had been put together with tiny hand stitches.

Later when everyone in Castle Doddard has turned in for the evening and I am sitting up in the four-poster bed writing my diary and thinking about fairies, I suddenly hear in the stillness of the night the sound of rhythmic sleeping snorts. It seems that Nigel is in restful slumber in a snore room on the floor above.

18

Up the Déise

Pam tells me at breakfast she is currently reading *The Fatal Shore* by Robert Hughes, about the early history of white Australia and the penal settlements. Given she is in her late-80s with no plans to visit Australia, I am amazed that she's reading such a detailed history. Pam is well-informed yet she is also great fun and continually thinks of others. Perhaps that's why she has a beautiful serenity about her. I also wonder if this peace comes from having grown up in India with its rich spiritual tradition, or the time she spends every year with her close friends in Pakistan, the Pataudis. Or maybe it's because she doesn't drink alcohol. Whatever it is she has a phenomenal fortitude which enables her to continue to cherish everything and everybody in her life. She knows what it's like to suffer, having lost her husband and second daughter, Penelope, but hasn't been diminished by this. Staying with her has truly been a joy and inspiration and I feel so lucky to have had this opportunity on my journey.

After breakfast I walk around the ornamental lake. It is an abundance of reeds and lilies and from the far side I get a magnificent view of the castle across the water. I also look at the tiny barrel-shaped painted wooden caravan that Pam and Steve lived in for two years while they were renovating Castle Doddard. When I first came to Ireland I would occasionally see a family of Irish Travellers sitting up behind a horse pulling one of these old caravans. But today, the travelling people of Ireland have succumbed to the comforts and luxuries of the far less romantic and much more modern and larger mobile homes.

Rather than immediately rejoining St Declan's Way and walking straight down to Lismore today, I have decided to walk to Mount Melleray, the famous Cistercian abbey not far from here. Pam tells me that the local children used to walk through the heather across the mountain to Melleray to school every day, but does not know exactly which way they went, so I decide to stick to the road.

It is eleven o'clock before I leave. Everyone congregates in the drive to see me off. Nigel, Alexandra and Marianne are driving through Lismore to the airport later today so I gratefully accept their offer to drop my backpack at Willoughby's Garage in Lismore on their way.

Pam has told me there is a track that goes up to the Cappoquin road which takes me to the turning to Mount Melleray. I assume it is the narrow path I've found, but then have to hop from tuft to tuft of heather to avoid the wet boggy ground. It is only after I trip and fall flat on my face in the bog that I notice a perfectly good track just to my left. Beside it a wood-speckled butterfly, a symbol of transformation and inspiration, is hovering above a single stem of orange-headed asphodel.

Almost immediately I find myself utterly delighted at being out here on the mountain in this vast expanse of nature. It is a clear day and I can see the top of the Knockmealdown itself. I think of all the times I've climbed it, and how often it has been shrouded in mist at the top.

Suddenly the morning silence is broken by a loud donkey bray which reverberates across the mountain's carpet of purple heather. There's a folktale that says at the time of creation no plant was willing to cover the bare mountain tops. Heather was a shy plant with no flowers, and feeling sorry for the mountains it covered them in its green. As a reward for its unselfish act, God granted heather its vibrant little flowers in abundance, so it could cover the mountains every autumn in a magnificent spread of purple.

Swallows dive and swoop in front of me as I walk along the mountain road. On the banks beside the road grow scabious, knapweed and blackberries. The blackberries turn out to be more appetising to look at than taste. One is watery, the next is sour—no doubt too much rain and not enough sun this summer—and I have to spit out five before I taste my first delicious blackberry of the day. A fuchsia bush in front of a cottage drips with its deep red flowers. Beside a stone wall there's Himalayan balsam with its long green leaves and pink flowers which look like the homes of small fairies.

I have hardly been walking an hour and my legs already ache. Despite being fairly fit I realise I'm not used to walking every day like this. Considering that my backpack has been travelling by car for the last three days, I hate to think what state I would be in if I'd been carrying it.

The road does a sharp zig-zag as it crosses the narrow Glenakeefe River bubbling down the mountain. Then I pass the track where St Declan's Way comes down from Bottleneck Pass. If Susie and I had managed to find our way over the mountain a couple of days ago, this is where we would have come out. Seeing it I immediately feel annoyed again that we had to turn back.

A year from now my cousin Charles and I followed this track, and on a clear sunny afternoon we traced the way up to Bottleneck Pass and down the Tipperary side of the mountain to where Susie and I reached in the mist. Because of the sheep tracks and the many gullies formed by rain runoff, it was hard for us to always see St Declan's Way. But there were moments when I knew for certain, as we followed a path with a bank on either side, that this was the ancient highway.

We made our way up to the pass, with skylarks swooping low over the heather, white tufts of bog cotton blowing in the breeze and the plaintive call of a curlew in the distance. Sheep bones cleaned by the weather lay between pieces of glittering white quartz and a flat woolly fleece rued a recent death, a reminder of how harsh conditions can be on the mountain.

We reached the pass to find a line of stones, which at intervals became a low dry stone wall, defining the county boundary between Tipperary and Waterford. On top of the wall secured by a large stone was a Liverpool football cap, faded pink from the weather, on which was written, 'You'll never walk alone'. The cap was certainly a long way from home. Liverpool is where many Irish emigrants ended up after crossing the Irish Sea to England. I couldn't help wondering who the cap belonged to and how it ended up there.

Below us the rolling plains of Tipperary stretched out into the distance. I could also see the tract of forestry from which Susie and I emerged onto the mountain. Up there, away from cars, houses and people, it was easy to imagine St Declan and his followers walking behind him as they made their way from Lismore to Cashel. But the most exhilarating moment was turning around and looking south over Waterford. There in the distance was the wide Blackwater River, a glistening shiny grey weaving through the land, and from that height St Declan's Way could be seen quite clearly carving its way through the heather.

Today, though, I continue along the road to Mount Melleray. On a stone wall the silky white beards of willowherb hang down below its pink flowers. Dotted here and there are rowans burgeoning with clusters of their magical red berries. In the far distance are the Comeragh Mountains. Like the Knockmealdowns they are a low undulating range that many people might consider more like hills than mountains. I turn a corner and away to the left I get my first glimpse of Mount Melleray, the huge grey stone building, with the purple Knockmealdown Mountains behind it.

It's ten to one when I reach the turning to Mount Melleray. Here at the T-junction of the two mountain roads, like an oasis in the desert, is the Cat's Bar.

Mount Melleray used to be a drying out place for alcoholics and those with a drinking problem. Men used to travel from all over Ireland to the monastery for the cure, and they would have their last drink here. It was also the first temptation when, a couple of weeks later, these men, having pledged never to drink again, emerged from the abbey.

At this T-junction they could turn left to Cappoquin, right to the Vee, or straight ahead into the Cat's Bar. There's a sign saying 'Food' and an arrow pointing to the side of the building. Hungry, I follow the sign around the pub to find an ashtray full of cigarette butts on a wooden table and the door locked. I'm about to walk away when a middle-aged man appears and lets me in. I sit at the bar and order a pot of tea and a toasted cheese and tomato sandwich. The man who's called Mike, tells me that his surname is Power, and that his father's family came here with the French, which I suppose means the Normans in the twelfth century. As I'm pondering how long you have to live in Ireland not to be considered a blow-in, he hurriedly adds his mother's side of the family are O'Keeffes and have owned the bar for five generations.

I am soon joined at the bar by a small man with a grey beard, who orders a pint of Guinness and sits under his tweed cap slowly drinking it. Having had a big night out until quarter to three, Michael is applying the hair of the dog to his hangover. He used to be a 'greasy monkey', which I discover is a mechanic, but is now on a Fas scheme, a government initiative to get unemployed people back into the workforce. He's working part-time looking after the scout hall at Mount Melleray. His father and grandfather also worked at Melleray, he adds. Then he tells me there are only 27 monks left at the abbey now and they are mostly old. Traditionally large Irish Catholic families sent one son into the priesthood, but few men nowadays are choosing this way of life.

The radio is on and the main news feature is that Cappoquin Chickens has gone into liquidation today. This local business rearing battery chickens employs 150 people full-time, and another 100 seasonally, so is the biggest employer in the area. This is a huge blow to the small community. Many local farmers have chicken houses, so the effect on the area's economy is likely to be enormous.

Michael tells me that Michael O'Connor, whose father started Cappoquin Chickens and whose two sons run it today, was in the hurling team 50 years ago when the Déise, the local Waterford team, won the All-Ireland series. He explains the Déise are in the All-Ireland hurling final at Croke Park in Dublin this Sunday playing against the Kilkenny Cats. The Cats are the favourites, having won the series for the last three years. The last time the Déise were in the finals was 45 years ago.

However, it is looking an auspicious year for the Déise, he tells me, because Frankie Walsh was captain when they won in 1959 and they also have a Walsh for captain this year. It's Michael Walsh, known as 'Brick Walsh'. There are three hurlers from Lismore, Dan Shanahan, known as 'Dan the Man', and nominated Hurler of the Year last year, as well as brothers Dave and Eoin Bennett.

Hurling has been an Irish pastime for at least 2000 years. Once described as 'two degrees safer than war', it is the world's fastest team game, and like much else in Ireland is intertwined with politics and also religion.

The Statutes of Kilkenny passed 650 years ago forbade the Normans, or Old English as they were known, to play hurling. The English crown believed they were becoming 'more Irish than the Irish'. It also forbade them to use Irish names, marry into Irish families, wear the Irish mode of dress, and use the Irish language and Irish laws.

Today hurling is played under the auspices of the Gaelic Athletic Association (GAA) and its local club structure is organised through the Roman Catholic parishes. The GAA was founded more than 100 years ago, and its first patron was Archbishop Thomas Croke of Cashel. I walked past the memorial to him half a dozen times while I was in Cashel. Croke Park, the Dublin ground at which the All-Ireland final is played, is named after him.

Tina, who brought me my lunch, is now standing behind the bar animatedly discussing the match with Michael. Obviously Tina's doing her best to make sure their lads win, as I notice a string of blue and white Déise flags hanging all along the back of the bar. Below the flags is a picture of the Pope clad in blue and white robes and holding a hurley up above his head. Underneath it says, 'Up the Déise. Don't Stop Believing.'

I suggest to Michael that as the Déise have the support of the Pope surely they are bound to win, to which he replies, 'Just because they have the Pope on their side doesn't mean they have God on their side.'

19

Moving statues

The turning opposite the Cat's Bar goes to Mount Melleray Abbey, and in a hollow just off this road is the Melleray Grotto. I can't resist the short detour. Standing on the hillside surrounded by bracken is a dazzling white statue of the Virgin Mary and nailed to a tree a sign reads, 'I am the Immaculate Conception'. Water from a spring gushes down the side of the hill and into a stone trough. Above it is a stone arch with two small pillars on either side of it. Half a dozen china mugs have been placed in the arched alcove of one of the pillars for people to drink the water. There's an intimacy about the place, but the gravel on the ground and the modern stonework also give it a municipal feeling.

This is no ordinary grotto. On the evening of Friday 16 August 1985, seventeen-year-old Ursula O'Rourke came with her family to the grotto to pray. On her way out, she looked up at the statue and noticed it was moving. She looked away several times to be sure she wasn't imagining it, then realised this was a vision of the Virgin Mary. She told her family and took them back to the statue—the vision was still there, but much fainter.

The following day people came to pray and many saw the statue change to Jesus Christ, Padre Pio and visions of other holy figures. On Sunday afternoon Michael Cliffe, whose farm is near Castle Doddard, came with his twelve-year-old son, Tom. Tom saw the face of Jesus Christ superimposed on the statue. A couple of hours later he came back with his mother to the grotto. This time he saw the statue moving, her cloak blowing in the wind. He then saw a silver crown appear on her head and golden hair flowing to her shoulders. Recognising this figure as the Virgin Mary, he heard her say, 'I want you'. This distressed Tom. He left the grotto saying to his mother he did not want to come back. That evening the Virgin Mary appeared to a local farmer and said, 'Preserve Sunday for prayer'.

Tom Cliffe did come back to the grotto and over the next six days he and his eleven-year-old cousin, Barry Buckley, saw numerous visions of the Virgin Mary and also heard her speak. At one stage she said, 'Behave', because people were talking and children were running about. The two boys could see and hear her, and relayed what she was saying to the increasing number of people gathering daily at the grotto. At one point the boys saw the Virgin Mary walk down some steps and come towards them with her arms outstretched, but when Tom put his hands out to touch her, she said, 'No!' and walked away from him.

The vision often asked for prayers to be said, and the boys could see and hear her also saying the rosary, but they noticed she never said 'Mary'. Often a decade of the rosary was said in Irish, and the boys realised that she, too, was speaking in Irish. One day the Virgin Mary asked for a hymn to be sung, which Tom and Barry did not know. They relayed the words and people recognised it as 'Peace is Flowing Like a River'.

After this the Virgin Mary said, 'I will make a movement to the people.' Then, not only the boys but also others began to see the statue's head move, then her finger, and finally they watched her turn towards the road where many people were gathered because there was no room for them in the grotto. That evening the Virgin Mother said she wanted the people out in the road to come in and see her because she would leave soon.

For the next two days, through the boys, the Virgin Mary asked for hymns and prayers. She asked people to pray harder and said, 'The world must improve and the world must believe.' Saturday 24 August was the last day that she spoke to the boys. The events at the Melleray Grotto came to an end. However, since then many people have reported seeing visions while praying at the grotto, including ones of Jesus Christ, Mary and many saints.

As I fill my bottle with water from the spring I think of the misfortune that has struck so many people associated with the visions here. A year after the apparitions Barry's older brother was killed in a road accident, and five years later Barry died in a motorcycle crash. Tom nearly died due to a critical illness, and his sister had two serious horseriding accidents.

Other people connected to the grotto have been struck early in life by incurable cancers. These occurrences have caused many people to surmise that the extraordinary ten-day event only brought bad luck, while others believe that it gave them the strength to endure the subsequent tragedies.

To the right of the spring is a nativity scene and next to it a big black box with 'Petitions Only' written on it in white paint. In a covered area there are several rows of church pews, and behind them on the back wall of the covered area are pictures of Mary and Jesus, statues, strings of rosary beads and notes pinned to a shelf. 'Lord, Cure Danny of his epilepsy if not relieve him. Paddy and Angela, Jacqui and Phil' one scrap of paper reads. On another is 'Michelle, I will always love you. Please forgive me. Love Yish'. 'I love you Mum and Dad. Dear Lord please keep everyone safe,' writes a little girl called Clodagh, ending her note with numerous kisses. I am very touched seeing these messages and they make me think about the power of faith and prayer and what support they can give people in their lives.

Two women and two men are sitting talking. Occasionally, one of the women pauses her chatter to the other woman and loudly asks her husband a question. I wonder whether the Virgin Mary will glide down and admonish them for lounging around gossiping, but she stands as resolutely immovable as ever. Down the hill from the car park comes a grey-haired man followed by a woman with a stick walking very slowly. Her left leg doesn't bend at all, and her left arm hangs down limply. I watch her as she takes some water from the well and crosses herself.

The statue here at Melleray Grotto was not the only one reported to have moved in Ireland in 1985. In February that year a seven-year-old girl was in St Mary's Church in Asdee in County Kerry when she saw the Sacred Heart crook his finger and beckon her over to him. Then she saw the Virgin Mary's mouth open. This wasn't an isolated experience. Other children were gathered in the church at the time, and 36 of them and many of their accompanying parents say they saw the statues move.

The statue which attracted the most visitors and an enormous amount of media attention was the Virgin Mary in the village of Ballinaspittle, County Cork. In late July of 1985 two teenage girls reported seeing the statue move. Within days thousands of people were gathering at the grotto every evening, joining in prayers being said over a PA system. Every night people claimed they saw the statue move. The statue's eyes were seen opening and closing, her hands were seen moving, and some people saw her rocking to and fro. Sometimes people said they saw the faces of other Christian figures, such as Jesus Christ or Padre Pio, superimposed on the statue.

Then a 37-year-old mother of four, Frances O'Riordan, who had been completely deaf since the age of twenty had her hearing restored during a visit to the Ballinaspittle grotto. A subsequent visit to an ear specialist confined that Frances now had 30 per cent of her hearing back. Another woman who had very painful arthritis in her feet and legs got up from praying to find the pain had completely disappeared.

Crowds gathered at the Ballinaspittle grotto for more than three months until two men destroyed the face and damaged the hands of the statue with a hammer and axe, and the statue was taken away to be repaired.

Theories abound as to why so many people were seeing the statue at Ballinaspittle move. Some people say it was an optical illusion caused by staring at the crown of eleven small electric lights which formed a halo around the statue's head. Others put it down to autosuggestion and mass hallucination.

Many people were quick to dismiss the moving statue epidemic in Ireland that year, saying it was purely hysteria and wild imagination. To me, it is much more mysterious, another instance of the thin veil between this world and another. I believe miracles and the mystical have continued to weave their way through everyday life. When one of the teenage girls was asked what she was thinking about just before she saw the statue move at Ballinaspittle, she replied, 'If I was thinking of anything it was about the good time we'd had at Cleo's Disco in Bandon the night before.'

20

The miraculous bin

Drivers wave to me as they pass me walking from the grotto to the abbey. People always used to wave when they passed each other on country roads and I love the acknowledgement, but now with more cars it is less common. I'm astonished by the number of houses along the road with blue and white Déise flags flying from their gates, or blue and white chequered bunting hanging from the eaves.

Halfway up the long tarmac drive to the abbey are a number of buildings, one of which says 'Scout activities' over the door. Apparently, these were built as boarding houses for students of Mount Melleray College, the school which the monks ran for 130 years. But for the last three decades, since the school closed, they have been leased to the Catholic Boy Scouts of Ireland.

Mount Melleray Abbey is a large grey building with that seeming impenetrable permanence that only ecclesiastical buildings have. I go to reception where Brother John, a thin monk in his early 40s, is dealing with enquiries and answering a busy telephone. He is wearing a black scapular over a long-sleeved ankle-length white habit and a thick brown leather belt. I wonder if the monks' garb has changed since the Cistercians were founded in 1098.

The abbey has a guesthouse and has been a retreat for many visitors over the years, including Daniel O'Connell, the tireless nineteenth-century Irish campaigner for Catholic emancipation. Another frequent visitor during his long presidency of Ireland was Eamon De Valera. In between telephone calls Brother John checks in a man staying at the abbey for a few days. Then another man arrives and says he wants to buy a mass—prayers to be said for a loved one. 'Living or dead?' Brother John asks him, 'Dead,' replies the man. So Brother John flicks through a box of cards before apologetically telling the man there are only living cards. Then he adds that actually cards for the living and the dead are the same. So the man takes a living card, pays 10 euros, then writes in it and puts it in an envelope.

One of the reasons I've come to the abbey is that I've heard about its 'miraculous bin' and am very keen to see it. Brother John explains this isn't possible as the bin is in the monks' private quarters. However, he does tell me the story. Abbot Vincent, who founded Mount Melleray Abbey, went away for a few months several years after it was established. Before he left he bought enough oatmeal to feed the community for a couple of weeks. He was asked by the prior what should be done when this grain ran out, and whether the monks should stop giving to the poor. Abbot Vincent's reply was to continue to give to the poor and trust in divine providence. So the monks followed his instructions and as a result all 90 monks and the poor were supplied with food from the grain bin for more than two months. After this miracle the bin was kept as a reminder of this extraordinary occurrence.

Abbot Vincent then made a rule that no poor person was ever to be sent away from Mount Melleray hungry. This was no idle undertaking. Though it was several years before the Great Potato Famine, which affected the whole country, this part of Ireland was facing famine. Not only were the monks providing for themselves, but also 60 to 70 people were being given food on a daily basis. On several occasions between 600 and 700 people received food from them in one day.

My friend Kieran Heffernan, the historian, told me that as a boy he went with his father to Mount Melleray to give thanks for the harvest and see the miraculous bin. He described it as a big timber thing, the size of the table. 'I remember a monk would be there and he would open it and we would all look in,' Kieran recollected. Folks would ask, 'How many people came?' And the monk would reply, 'Thousands of people came to be fed, and the monks scooped out the corn and gave it to them and the bin never emptied.'

When he was older Kieran discovered the monks had another property in Tipperary, which they had to sell to pay for all the corn they had bought to feed the poor, as after the famine they had huge debts to pay. Having discovered this Kieran told his father he didn't think it was a miraculous bin at all. 'Nonsense,' old man Heffernan replied, 'of course it's miraculous.'

The Cistercians dedicate their daily lives to seeking God through prayer, work and sacred reading. The order is based on the Rule of St Benedict, which said that a monastery should be made up of a stable and enclosed community whose daily activities are divided between work, worship, reading and rest. St Benedict believed the goal of a monk is the perfect love of God, which is expressed in the practice of obedience, silence, humility, service of others and 'preferring nothing whatever to Christ'. The Cistercians were founded in France more than nine hundred years ago by a group of Benedictine monks wanting to follow the Rule of St Benedict more strictly. At the time of King Henry VIII's dissolution of the monasteries, there were 34 Cistercian monasteries in Ireland.

Founded 180 years ago Mount Melleray was the first monastery to be established in Ireland after the Catholic emancipation. The abbey was established here because the monks received an offer from Sir Richard Keane of Cappoquin offering them a 99-year lease for 470 acres of barren waste-land, known as *Scrahan*, meaning 'the coarse land', on the Knockmealdowns.

With the help of hundreds of men from local surrounding parishes, they slowly reclaimed 120 acres of the mountain and made it suitable for growing crops. Often a dozen men were needed to walk in front of the plough, picking up stones, and every stone was put aside for the building of the abbey itself.

A year after the foundation stone was laid for the abbey, its abbot, Father Vincent, was having to turn young men away because the monastery was so crowded but today there are fewer than 30. Near the entrance to the abbey itself is a notice entitled, 'To become a monk', and underneath is written, 'Do you have a desire for prayer? Are you seeking a community that will support and accompany you in your efforts to live a deeper life of prayer? Perhaps Mount Melleray is that community.'

As I think about the abbey's dwindling numbers, I am approached by a very cheerful elderly monk wearing a black skullcap. He introduces himself as Father Bonaventure and asks what brings me here. When I tell him I am walking St Declan's Way, he replies he's pleased I'm enjoying the outdoor life. I also mention that while I'm in Lismore I shall be spending some time with the Cistercian nuns at St Mary's Abbey, Glencairn. He used to be the chaplain there, and asks me to pass on his regards to them.

Before I leave the abbey, I go into the gift shop and buy a book mark for Stephen. The monk at the counter must be at least 90 years old and looks as if he might doze off in between customers. The shop is empty except for me on this quiet Monday afternoon. Pam had mentioned that taking the abbey's back drive onto the main road would save me quite a bit of walking, so I ask the monk for directions. He explains I need to go out past the abbey cemetery and in a slow shaky hand he draws me a map on a brown paper bag.

As I take one last look at the huge grey edifice I am overcome with gloom. The monks I met were friendly, but to me the place feels cold and austere. I thought visiting this religious community would make me feel uplifted but it's the reverse. Then I remember feeling the same way when we came up here, as a family, years ago for midnight mass.

At first I think it's because I feel I can't relate to this all-male world. Despite my admiration for these monks leading their strict life of work and prayer, and also for what the abbey has achieved over the years, I just can't connect with them. But on reflection I realise it was the same earlier today at the grotto. In both instances I simply don't feel part of what is represented here. Although my spirit aches to belong, instead I feel like an outside observer. So once more I'm wondering what I'm doing here, and questioning what it is I'm looking for.

21

Limping in halfway

I follow the old monk's directions and take the track past the cemetery with its scattering of headstones. I've barely been walking ten minutes when I wish I had visited the monastery tea room and had something stodgy and sweet to eat. I feel tired and in need of energy for the 7-mile walk to Lismore. Instead I pick a handful of blackberries growing among the rosehips in the hedgerows, and then remember the apple in my bag that Barbara picked for me from a tree at Castle Grace. Taking a large bite I realise how special it is to be eating this fruit picked straight from the tree, rather than buying an apple from a supermarket that might have been grown a thousand miles away and sat in cold storage for a couple of months before being put on the shelf.

It's just after five o'clock when I rejoin St Declan's Way, now a narrow mountain road that runs through farmland interspersed with the occasional modern bungalow. Dogs bark fiercely from the gardens and yards, or come out onto the road woofing loudly until they get close enough to sniff me. Then a black cat runs across the road ahead. It is believed to be a sign of bad luck, they say, when a black cat crosses your path. Given how exhausted I am, remembering this old superstition makes me feel a bit nervous.

After an old stone bridge over the Glenakeefe River there is a fork in the road. I take the left turning and walk up the hill. I'm hoping to find the site of the Shrubbery of the Lepers, which apparently was a spa for the sick. Two collies emerge barking from a modern house. A woman opens the sliding front door at the sound of the dogs. When I ask her about the Shrubbery of the Lepers, she says she hasn't heard of it, but invites me in.

Where am I from, is her first question. I tell her I used to live in Lismore. When I say my surname is Burton, she asks if my father is 'Mr Burton from the castle'. It turns out her late husband knew my father well. She introduces herself as Kathleen Colman. Then her daughter, Patricia, appears from the sitting room with her boisterous two-year-old son. They have been watching the evening news. The main story is about Cappoquin Chickens going into administration. One of their relatives works there. 'The company only has an eight million euro debt,' Patricia says optimistically, 'that's not much to get over.'

They urge me to sit down and have coffee. I long to accept but I'm worried that if I were to sink into one of the enticing sofas I might never get up. Patricia tells me she is driving into Lismore shortly and can give me a lift. Both mother and daughter are very persuasive. Even though I explain I am determined to walk, I can see that they know it is just a question of a little more cajoling. So before I succumb to the temptation I say goodbye and press on.

Back on the road I pass clumps of watercrowfoot with its white petals and yellow centres where they're growing in the wet verge opposite a farmhouse. Just beyond here St Declan's Way turns up a muddy boreen and onto a narrow footpath. Briars form an arch above my head and it's like walking through a tunnel of green. The path comes out near a house on another narrow road. I am now passed by an occasional car and a few tractors before I find myself in the townland of Ballyrafter, high on the hill looking down on Lismore and the wide Blackwater River snaking through the valley below. It's so exciting to see them and to know I'll soon be there. At this point Patricia pulls up beside me in her four-wheel drive, and still baffled as to why anyone would walk when they could drive, offers me a lift the rest of the way into town. Again I am tempted to get into the passenger seat but decline.

At the bottom of the hill I join the main road down from the mountain. I pick up my horribly heavy backpack, which Nigel, Alexandra and Marianne dropped off at the garage for me and walk slowly towards the bridge.

The sight of Lismore Castle rising up from the banks of the Blackwater is always breathtaking and as usual awakens memories in me of when we lived there. But it feels particularly special this evening because I have arrived here on foot. As I stare at this magnificent building with its mass of turrets, chimneys and castellated towers, I notice, much to my surprise and delight, flying from the flag tower is the blue and white Déise flag.

I look down at the inches. I remember learning to fly-fish here below the bridge the summer we after came to Lismore. Joe Dooley taught me. He was a short stocky man who used to check fishing licences and could always be seen on the banks of the river with a curl of smoke under his tweed fishing hat. It was his great patience which eventually enabled me to cast a line. He would take the rod in his nicotine-stained fingers and with a slight flick the line would unfurl perfectly, barely rippling the water, and he'd place the fly effortlessly within a foot or so of the far bank. My line never landed with such finesse and, despite hours of casting on this bit of bank, I never caught a fish here.

I did, however, catch a trout one evening at Fort William further upriver. A group of us were casting away in between nips of poteen when I felt a tug and thought I had hooked something. The response from the others was that my line was probably caught on the bottom. But despite the cynicism of my fellow fishermen I landed that small fish and ate it the following morning for breakfast.

Maybe my attempts to fish below the castle were so unsuccessful because the dogs always liked to go swimming at the same time, but, actually, I didn't care whether I caught a fish or not. I used to love coming down here with my father in the early evening for an hour or so of fishing, because I cherished the stillness at that time of day. I loved standing in the shallows quietly casting, watching the river and listening to the water running across the stones and the breeze rustling the trees. I remember one evening there was an otter playing on the opposite bank. We sat and watched it diving into the river, then clambering along the edge of the water before taking another plunge. Just when we thought it had disappeared, its black sleek head would re-emerge and look around, before heading to the bank, scurrying over the rocks and taking another dip.

I cross the bridge and walk up Ferry Lane to the main street of Lismore. A couple of teenage girls say hello as I pass them. Willy Roche's supermarket is still open, but the town is quiet.

For the next few days I am staying with old friends Nick and Alison Trigg, who live a mile and a half out of Lismore along the road to Tallow. The thought of having to walk that far is agonising, so I'm cheered and relieved when I ring them from the telephone box opposite the post office and Alison offers to come and pick me up.

I am hobbling slowly out of town when she pulls up and in a booming voice immediately tells me that I look lame. If I were a horse she definitely would not have taken me hunting today, she declares.

Tourtane is a pretty Georgian house. When we arrive Nick appears on the front door step with Flora, the Triggs' elderly golden retriever who farts. I adore Alison and Nick. They met when he was at Oxford, and she was only eighteen when they married. Despite constantly swearing at and arguing with one another for nearly 50 years, their love for each other is tangible. They also both have a great interest in other people, and I can't count how many times I have sat at their kitchen table and been listened to and given advice on whatever the current problem was in my life.

Their sons, Charles and James, are friends of my cousins and mine, and we all used to party together in our late teens and early twenties. James and I also spent much of our summer holidays together, playing tennis, swimming or fishing. These days Charles lives with his wife, Elaine, and their three children in the back part of the house.

Nick first came to Ireland when he was thirteen, having grown up in India where his father was Conservator of Forests for Bengal, and he used to travel with his parents and governess on large steam launches up the Ganges and Pranaputra rivers. They had their own elephants which he used to wash everyday. After India's independence his father no longer had a job, so the family moved to Chicester in the south of England. His father soon found Chicester dull, so decided to move the family to Ireland. There was an advertisement in the personal column of *The Times* listing the wing of Cappoquin House for rent, and so they moved there.

That summer Nick learnt to fly-fish and describes taking a boat with his father and a gilly from Bull Sod, near the Round Hill, the Iron Age fort downstream of Lismore, and spending the day drifting down to Cappoquin fishing for trout. Three or four times he went fishing on the boat with his father that summer. Then only four months after they had arrived, his father was out shooting one day and had a massive heart attack and died.

Nick's mother decided to stay in Ireland and remained in the wing of Cappoquin House. Sir Richard Keane, whose predecessor leased the Cistercian monks the land on the mountain, and is now 99 years old, became like a surrogate father to him.

Nick, Alison and I sit at the kitchen table eating supper. I'm proud as punch at having made it to Lismore, more than halfway along St Declan's Way, and I tell them about my travels so far. But later as I creep like an old woman, stiff and sore, upstairs to bed, part of me continues to question why on earth I'm on this pilgrimage? I still don't know what I hope to achieve and wonder whether there's any point to it at all.

But then I remember that I was contemplating turning back a couple of miles out of Cashel. Now, although I am tired and sore from the walking, I've relaxed into another way of being. Every day it is a joy to reach my destination, but what I love most about this journey is the walking. For once in my life I'm going at a pace that allows me to really appreciate my surroundings. There's time to take note of what's growing in the hedgerows, time to smell the honeysuckle, or to stop and pick a few blackberries.

This last week I have had the opportunity to connect with the land I am walking through in a way that is quite different to when you go for a walk for just an hour or two. I guess, if I'm being honest, time-out like this is a rare privilege for me and probably would be for most people in this fast-paced world. As I walk St Declan's Way I have slowed down. For these few precious days I'm immersed in a different world. My thoughts have slowed down. I'm less anxious about outcomes. Even my interactions with friends are different. Before this I have always only been for meals or drinks with the Grubbs,

Pam Stevenson and the Triggs, but staying with people means getting to know them much better. An even greater gift than being given a meal, is staying with friends in their home, and being part of the daily tapestry of their lives.

All that I have seen and all the interactions in the last seven days have been imbued with the many gifts that come from slowness, like being in step with the natural rhythm of life. As I set off each day I don't have endless deadlines to meet or phone calls to make, all that's required of me is to reach my next destination along the way.

As I reach the top stair and limp along the landing I realise I have stepped off the treadmill. I run myself a deep hot bath. The luxury of it is indescribable. I'm so exhausted I nearly fall asleep while lying in it, so I drag myself out and make for bed, feeling incredibly grateful to have this opportunity.

22

The Tallow Horse Fair

The next I know I hear the grandfather clock at the bottom of the stairs chime eight. As I lie in bed I watch the house martins circling outside the window. They swoop towards the glass, looking as if they are going to fly straight through it, but at the last moment they twist and dive away. I'm still stiff and sore when I get up, but doing some yoga helps.

The kitchen of this attractive 200-year-old stone house is immediately to the left of the front door. The kitchen table sits in the middle of the room between the large Georgian window and the Aga. It is the most conducive place for talking. I linger here, chatting and eating pieces of Alison's homemade soda bread toasted on the Aga and drinking mugs of weak Lady Grey tea. Eventually Alison says, 'Right', in that definite way which precedes getting on with a day. Nick disappears to his office and I realise I'd better get moving.

Despite the fact that she is looking for a pony for her grandson Baz, Alison can't be persuaded to come with me to the Tallow Horse Fair today. She says she's scared that she would end up buying a four-legged beast, which would be quite likely to have some dreadful quirk that would put Baz off riding for life. Given she told me last night that her mother bought two donkeys on the quay in Cork before getting on the ferry back to England, I can see that she might have a genetic tendency towards impulse buying, but on the other hand if she is looking for a pony a horse fair isn't a bad place to find one.

Alison has a good eye for a horse. She once bought a hunter from the Tallow Fair which she rode for fifteen years. He was a good horse, except that he would rear up when he had had enough, and no matter what she did she couldn't break this habit. She goes on to tell me that the calibre of horses being sold today are not what they were. At that moment her son Charles sticks his head through the kitchen window and adds disparagingly that the Tallow Horse Fair is 'now just a lot of knackers and tinkers'.

Undeterred I'm looking forward to today. For me this annual event epitomises the Irish love of the horse and I wouldn't miss it for the world. Ireland's most well-known horse fair is at Ballinasloe in County Galway, which was first held more than 300 years ago. The Tallow Fair has been going for more than a century. As well as drawing anyone wanting to buy or sell horses, or who is up for a good day out and catching up with friends, the fairs also attract Ireland's travelling people who are great horse dealers.

Known in Irish as *an Lucht Siúil*, 'the walking people', Irish Travellers are believed to be descended from those made homeless by Oliver Cromwell's military campaign in Ireland and later during the Great Famine. Not only do Irish Travellers have their own customs, but also their own language known as Gammon. It is thought to stem from Irish, but with words reversed, consonants transposed or a cluster of sounds added to the beginning or end of the word. Recently, modern slang and Romani words have also been added.

It's several miles to Tallow and also pouring with rain this morning. So I set off in my full wet-weather outfit: the broad-brimmed brown leather hat of my father's, the Gortex jacket a friend has lent me, and the plastic trousers Stephen's mother gave me, which Stephen used to wear when he was about twelve. As horse floats rattle past me along the main road, I quickly realise that Stephen's trousers are not waterproof, and am tempted to hitch a lift. But I press on and the sun has come out by the time I reach Tallow Hill.

As I walk down towards the town, I can see horse floats parked all along the Fermoy road and in the field beside the Bride River. The town has been closed to traffic and stalls have been set up on either side of the street, selling bridles and saddles, clothes, rugs, drills and also umbrellas. On one stand are two pink children's bicycles for sale. On another is a large sign saying 'Reading Glasses' and a selection of spectacles. An old man has a stall selling walking sticks he has made. Next to him is a huge catering truck selling burgers and chips, while a woman sits in a caravan opposite advertising 'fortune telling'. A Pakistani man, who tells me he lives in Gorey in

County Wexford and goes back to Pakistan once a year, is selling the Déise blue and white scarves, banners and flags. He's conversing loudly in Urdu to a fellow Pakistani with a coat and rug stall opposite.

I walk up the street with a couple who have come from Kilmacthomas near Waterford City. They tell me they have seen some good children's ponies. I wonder if I should ring Alison, but decide against it.

As we near the middle of the town the number of horses on parade increases. A jumpy black horse is skitting from one side of the street to the other. A man leads it round in circles in an effort to calm it, while unfazed passersby give them both a wide berth. Neat-looking teenage girls in riding hats ride their well-groomed mounts up and down the street. Two Traveller boys come bowling through bareback on a couple of shaggy ponies.

A sudden heavy shower of rain sends everyone running for shelter. Continuing up the street I see three ruddy-faced men peering out of the narrow window of a small horse float to see if the downpour is easing.

When I reach the centre of town there are so many horses and people it's hard to move. A man in a long brown raincoat and broad-brimmed hat is tethering two horses, while holding a part-beagle puppy under his coat, which he is also selling. Another man wearing a wide hat rides through the crowd on a large chestnut hunter. Five horses are tethered to a copper beech tree next to the undertakers. A couple of large men are holding the smallest ponies I have ever seen. Sturdy coloured tinker cobs with their feathered legs and thick manes and tails are paraded up and down. Then someone hits the flanks of a horse in his way, which causes a ripple of horses and hooves all the way up the street as they shunt forward.

I have arranged to meet my friend Alix at the stone horse monument in the middle of Tallow. So I climb up onto a concrete platform near it to see if I can see her in the crowd. Also standing there is a man with a video camera. He's taking footage of proceedings. It turns out he is from Tallow, but he quickly makes it clear he is not greatly in favour of its annual horse fair. He tells me there are no official organisers and as a result no one is responsible for the event. As I watch mothers blithely manoeuvre young children in their strollers up the street with horses sidestepping and kicking in every direction, I quietly rejoice that the Irish love of horses has prevailed over the fear of injury and public liability.

Alix arrives and we go into the Latch for lunch. The small low-ceilinged restaurant is packed full of people. We sit on the same table as a man called Pat Noonan from County Limerick. He's here today because he is selling a two-year-old horse, which someone is minding for him while he eats. He has a round red face and twinkly blue eyes. He tells us he hunts with the Scarteen during the week on a Tuesday or a Thursday because there'll only be about 70 horses in the hunt, as opposed to 150 on Saturday. It transpires that he knows Father Foley, a friend of Alix's mother. He gave Father Foley some goats. Father Foley, Alix explains, had a very happy life hunting with the Tipperary, until the church moved him to Dublin.

Pat Noonan works at the donkey sanctuary in Limerick. He tells us it's easy work, though initially he did get kicked a great deal. The sanctuary's most recent acquisition, he says, is a donkey who smokes. The donkey belonged to a man in his 80s, who was too old to look after the animal so gave it to the sanctuary. Apparently, the old man and the donkey used to share a pipe or cigarette together. As the donkey has only been separated from its owner for a few days, it's still looking for its nicotine fix. The donkey definitely inhales, Pat adds, because when someone gave it a cigarette the smoke came out of its nostrils.

The sun has come out by the time we leave the restaurant. The street is emptier and more people look as if they are engaged in serious sales transactions. Older men lean on sticks while young men pull on their cigarettes as they all watch the horses being led or ridden up and down the street. In the main square a man with three piebalds of varying sizes and a tall chestnut all tied to one rope walk together back and forth. Alix is jostled to one side as a horse and rider trot past.

A man from Ballyrafter selling donkeys says he has just refused an offer of 550 euros for four of them, including a dark brown eleven-day-old foal, as he earlier sold two for 1200 euros. Women in their caravans try to lure us in to have our fortunes told. A young man with red hair and freckles and penetrating blue eyes leans against a beautiful young grey mare. He only brought her in from the field yesterday, he tells us, and had a bit of trouble getting her into the horse float. He says we can have her for 1000 euros, and as we leave he brings the offer quickly down to 800.

Walking out of town back towards the bridge we come across a stall selling 100 per cent waterproof trousers for 10 euros, so I buy a pair. The Pakistani man selling Déise gear smiles as we go past. As I ponder on all the different nationalities that now live in Ireland compared to twenty years ago, we are serenaded by a group of Peruvian musicians selling their CDs from a stand—they are playing a stirring rendition of *Mull of Kintyre* on their wooden flutes and pipes.

The last time I went to the Tallow Horse Fair I was nineteen. It was part of the week-long Tallow Festival back then. One evening there was a rodeo and a group of us decided to enter. The boys were given bullocks to ride and the girls heifers. The boys were thrown from their bullocks almost instantly but somehow, by hanging onto the rope tied around the bucking beast's middle and gripping very hard with my knees, I managed to remain on a heifer until the bell rang, which was after six seconds, plus a second or two longer. As a result I came third and was bought numerous drinks in the pub.

The person who plied me most with drinks that night was Peter Magnier, who had recently given me his five-year-old hunter Barney to ride. I had next to no riding experience and am not very tall, and at 17 hands Barney was a very large horse. The first day I got on him I was catapulted into a bramble bush. On later occasions when I was riding through the Lismore woods Barney often got the bit between his teeth, and bolted. I used to slide off while he was going full pelt, terrified that otherwise I would be thrown off onto the tarmac when he reached the road.

Peter, meanwhile, thought it was marvellous that Barney was getting some exercise, and whenever I began to explain my latest mishap he would always pre-empt it by saying that Barney was a real gentleman. The evening of the rodeo in Tallow I think Peter was delighted to see that his horse's new rider had the ability to really grip with her knees—something I had quickly learnt from riding Barney.

23

Saints, sinners and a fur stole

My focus today is on history rather than horses and I am meeting the Dean of Lismore this morning at 11 a.m. to learn from him about the early history of the town. Before my appointment with the dean I decide to visit the Towers, a couple of miles out of Lismore. I used to come here with my mother to pick blackberries, but, as I follow the path through the woodlands, I see the brambles have been cut back and the place tidied up, so the fruit is less abundant.

I walk up the track until I come to the ornate Gothic archway and its distinctive gatehouses, with their castellated towers and turrets. I pass through the archway and down to the triple-arched stone bridge with its buttresses and parapets, and high-towered gate lodges at either end.

Even when I first saw this impressive construction, it seemed an excessive amount of masonry to cross the small stream gurgling and bubbling below. I assumed there must be an enormous house or castle at the end of the driveway, and was eager to get a glimpse of the home which had such an ostentatious approach. Much to my disappointment there was nothing there. Later I discovered the house had been demolished.

These extraordinary towers were built by Elizabeth, the wife of landowner Arthur Kiely-Ussher. Two hundred years ago he inherited 8000 acres here at Ballysaggartmore. Elizabeth's sister was married to Arthur's brother and they lived in the dreamy Strancally Castle overlooking the Blackwater River further downstream. However, towards the end of building Strancally Castle the money had run out, so gate houses were never constructed. After ten years of marriage Elizabeth finally managed to persuade her husband to allow her to draw up plans for a home of her dreams. Determined to outdo her sister she decided she needed not one but two impressive gate lodges. Her gardener was an artistic man who knew a great deal about architecture. He immediately began work on the ostentatious lodges and gates. No expense was spared on the design and materials. But just when work was to start on building the castle of her dreams, Arthur told her he had no more money. Much to her humiliation Elizabeth continued to live in the very plain house in Ballysaggartmore at the end of the avenue with its majestic entrances.

During the Great Famine Arthur Kiely-Ussher treated his tenants abominably and turned hundreds of starving families off his land. This, and the utter folly of these edifices, always makes me feel the Towers are worth visiting for curiosity more than anything else, and, despite the pretty woodlands and the stream, it's not a place I've ever wanted to linger for very long.

Returning to Lismore, I walk up Church Avenue, the pathway which runs between the castle and the cathedral. It is the mid-morning break for the small Church of Ireland school next to the cathedral. As I stand on the doorstep of the deanery waiting for the door to open, I watch a group of boys kicking a football around the schoolyard.

Dean Beare, who I have arranged to meet, is originally from West Cork. He's known locally as the 'Singing Bear' because of his love of choral music. He's a kind man and I have a lot to thank him for. A couple of months before my father died from cancer, the two of us were the only members of the congregation at Fountain, the little church near my parents' cottage outside Lismore. I wondered whether Dean Beare would give the service for only my father and me. But he did. He told us that it might look as if there were only three of us here, but actually the church was full of angels.

I think of his words often and they always make me smile. The Celts thought our world and the spirit one were interconnected and St Declan often acted on the guidance of angels. I believe angels communicate with the divine within us and help us to fulfil our potential.

The dean and I sit at a small table near the front door. He tells me he will be 75 in a couple of months. He is retiring and moving to Cork. I ask him to tell me about the early Christian church in Lismore. But before he does, he is adamant I understand that Christianity was in Ireland at least 100 years before St Patrick. Later I speak to Máire B de Paor, also known as Sister Declan, and author of several books on Gaelic Christianity. She says that Old Parish, in the Gaeltacht—the Irish speaking region—on the coast near Ardmore, is believed to be where the first Christians settled in Ireland. They were persecuted on the Continent so sailed here from Gaul and lived as shepherds. They had no church, but gathered together and said mass at a local well.

Having been worried when setting out from Cashel that I was walking St Declan's Way in the wrong direction, I'm delighted when the dean assures me that the ancient highway was travelled in both directions. It was used not only by pilgrims, but everyone going between Cashel, Lismore and Ardmore.

The Christian community in Lismore was founded nearly 1400 years ago when St Carthage, also known as St Mochuda, invited by the Prince of the Déise, came to Lismore. He built a church here on the hill where the cathedral stands today and founded a monastery on the site of the present-day castle. Very quickly Lismore became a major religious centre. The monastery continued to grow and 100 years later it was one of the main centres of learning in Europe.

Lismore's days of ecclesiastical glory did not last due to the numerous raids by the marauding Vikings and being plundered and burnt many times. However, it still remained an important religious centre in Ireland and St Malachy, who was responsible for bringing the Cistercian Order to Ireland, came and studied at Lismore. But 500 years after St Carthage founded the monastery, it seems that standards had dropped and Malachy described having been sent not to men, but to beasts. He claimed the monks were impious in their faith, shameless in their morals, wild, undisciplined and unclean, and more like pagans than Christians.

Malachy had died before King Henry II's visit to Ireland in 1171 which not only sealed the fate of the Celtic church, bringing it under the subjection of Rome, but also was the first step towards England's domination of Ireland.

It wasn't only the Irish clergy who submitted to Henry II's sovereignty, but also many of the Irish chieftains. The chieftains hoped for protection from the English king from the Norman warlords who were taking over vast tracts of land in Ireland. At the same time Henry forced the Norman warlords to accept him as their overlord.

A year later Strongbow plundered Lismore and this, plus another Norman attack the following year, completely destroyed the church and the monastery as well as the convent for women and the leper hospital here.

Henry II never went back to Ireland, but his visit was the start of England's control over Ireland. Later, he transferred all his rights as Lord of Ireland to his youngest son, and thirteen years after Henry II's visit Prince John came to Ireland and during his eight-month stay built the original castle at Lismore.

Unlike most of the other Churches of Ireland along St Declan's Way, the doors of St Carthage Cathedral are always open. Our footsteps on the stone floor echo up to the brightly painted vaulted roof and down the long nave where a couple of tourists are looking at the memorial stones in commemoration of members of the great university here 1200 years ago.

The dean has offered to show me a sheela-na-gig. He unlocks a door in the side chapel and then with another large key opens the arched wooden door to the library. Along the walls are high bookcases, the tops of which are castellated, and divided by what looks like a small wooden replica of the cathedral spire. The shelves are full of old, leather-bound books, which mostly contain sermons, the Dean tells me, pulling one out to show me. It was printed 150 years ago and the pages are uncut.

The sheela-na-gig, says the dean, was found in the churchyard in Tallow. Only the top half of it remains and disappointingly all I can make out carved in the block of stone is a bald-headed, flat-chested figure with a crooked arm.

He also unlocks the large parish chest. When I was in the cathedral library a couple of years ago, Adele Astaire's fur stole was lying in the bottom of the chest. Adele Astaire married Lord Charles Cavendish, the younger brother of the ninth Duke of Devonshire. They lived at Lismore and her brother, the dancing legend Fred Astaire, was a regular visitor. I've been told that Adele and he used to dance on the castle parapets, and imagine them toe-tapping up on the rooftops.

I asked the dean what the stole was doing there, to which he replied, 'I don't quite know. It was here before I came.' Then obviously rather irritated by this unreligious item taking up space in the parish chest, he asked if I would like it. I did wonder whether I, too, could do the soft shoe shuffle if I had this heirloom draped across my shoulders, but decided the fur and I would not make good partners, so declined the offer. Today, the fur is not in the chest, so he must have eventually found a home for it.

24

Lismore Castle

My next stop in town is Ken Madden, the real estate agent who sold my parents' cottage last year. 'Business is very quiet,' he tells me, 'house prices have dropped considerably.' Looking at me hopefully, he adds, 'It's a good time to buy.' The bust after the incredible boom of the Celtic Tiger is biting deep.

Ken's parents used to have a grocery shop and a bar further up the main street. Then he and his two brothers turned the whole premise into a pub. Now his sisters-in-law have opened a shop and café called the Summerhouse. I decide to go there for lunch and a cup of coffee. The food is homemade and good, but as I sit looking at the rack of organic wine and the shelves packed with jars of homemade jam, as well as coffee plungers, whisks and wooden spatulas, it makes me think of much the town has changed.

Lismore used to be rather a sleepy place, but now it's a 'heritage' town with an information centre. And, of course, with the passing years many businesses have closed down or changed. The little bar on Ferry Lane which sold bicycle tyres and inner tubes has now closed. The arcade, where I once went to buy a pair of tennis shoes and, because there were none in my size, it was suggested pragmatically that I buy a much larger size that was in stock and cut the toes off, has long since gone.

O'Brien's Bar, which Miss Casey owned and where she used to preside in the evening once her day behind the archaic typewriter in the castle office was over, is now O'Brien's Chop House. Miss Casey used to have packets of sugar and cans of peas neatly arranged on the wooden shelves above the bottles of spirits behind the bar. It was always quiet inside and there were never more than one or two other people on the couple of times I went in. The Chop House still has the bar, but the rest of the premise is now a restaurant. It's a good food haven which attracts people from more than an hour's drive away and does a roaring trade in Sunday lunch.

Now every June Lismore hosts the Immrama Festival of Travel Writing, and its program includes great travel writers such as Jan Morris, explorer Sir Ranulph Fiennes and BBC reporter Kate Adie. Occasionally, Lismore's own travel writer, Dervla Murphy, who has lived in Lismore all her life, also speaks. She cycled alone from Ireland to India in her 30s and wrote *Full Tilt*. Now in her 70s and many books later, including the wonderful *The Island that Dared* about Cuba, she is still riding her bicycle. She abhors modernity and is appalled that in recent years people in Lismore instead of walking are getting into their cars to drive short distances around town.

I head past the ornate monument in the middle of town, erected in memory of Archdeacon Ambrose Power for his generosity to the poor, and walk down the castle drive.

Halfway along the drive which is flanked either side by high stone walls is the seventeenth-century riding house. It was built originally to accommodate a couple of horsemen, who used to be on guard in two recesses in the narrow archway. In the riding house is a woman I don't know. She's collecting money from a couple who want to have a quick look around the castle gardens before they close. I walk up to the gatehouse tower with its pointy red roof. I wish I could just let myself in but the thick wooden entrance gates are firmly closed. Tom and Ann Brennock live in the gate lodge, and when I ring the doorbell Ann opens the gate for me.

The Brennocks moved into the gate lodge the first summer we were at Lismore. Ann is the castle gatekeeper and Tom works in the estate's woodlands. He is just home from work and is sitting at the table reading the paper. After filling me in on the castle news, Ann asks if I would like to walk around the garden. Louise, her daughter, says she and her golden retriever, Abbey, will come with me. Louise is in her last year of school. She has her mother's small stature and seems utterly unconscious of her natural beauty, her thick dark brown hair, vibrant blue eyes, clear fair skin and rosy cheeks.

In the courtyard I look across at the blue arched door at the base of the tower which used to be our front door and instantly remember the large key we had to open it. Louise and I enter the upper garden and wander through the greenhouse, where tomatoes are growing and red and brown onions are lying out to dry. In the top corner of the garden we climb up to the tower. This was a favourite spot of mine until I discovered it is called the Broghill Tower, after Lord Broghill, a great friend and follower of Oliver Cromwell. Broghill played a brutal part in the atrocities Cromwell meted out in Ireland, which caused the death or exile of 20 per cent of Ireland's population.

However, I still can't help loving the view from here of the hedges and neat flower beds of the terraced garden, laid out more than four centuries ago, and beyond it the castle and cathedral. When I ask Louise how long the Déise colours have been flying from the flag tower, she tells me after Tipperary lost to Waterford in the All-Ireland hurling semi-finals, Denis Nevin, the butler and clerk of works at the castle, originally from Tipperary, was made to hoist the Déise flag. She is going up to Dublin with her sister to see the match on Sunday. Because of this monumental occasion her school is closed on Monday.

Walking down towards the riding house we pass a bed of red and white tobacco flowers. I learnt at school that it was Sir Walter Raleigh who was responsible for first bringing tobacco and potatoes back from America. Raleigh first came to the attention of Queen Elizabeth I in 1580, when he helped suppress the Irish Desmond Rebellion. He quickly became a firm favourite of the queen. As a result, she always refused him permission to head an expedition, in case something happened to him. So for many years he never set foot on North American shores, but only organised landing parties and colonies there.

However, being the queen's favourite paid off in other ways. Sir Walter Raleigh leased Lismore Castle from the Bishop of Lismore. He later acquired it in full and was also given 42 000 acres by Queen Elizabeth. This included woodlands and mineral mines, and also the valuable Blackwater fishing rights. Raleigh was given these lands for fighting against the Earl of Desmond, Gerald FitzGerald and his allies, who were opposed to English rule in Ireland. When the earl was eventually killed, the Virgin Queen, as Elizabeth I was known, gave his land to Englishmen, hoping that the presence of loyal English settlers in Munster would end the troubles in this part of Ireland.

When in Ireland Sir Walter Raleigh spent a lot of time at Myrtle Grove, his house in the coastal town of Youghal, downstream from Lismore at the estuary of the Blackwater. The story goes that he was sitting in the garden smoking a pipe of his recently discovered tobacco, and one of his servants thought he was on fire and dowsed him with a bucket of water. It is also believed that potato plants collected on one of Raleigh's North American expeditions were planted at Myrtle Grove. Little did he know then what effect those plants with their tuber roots were to have on the future of Ireland.

Sir Walter Raleigh sold Lismore Castle and its estates to Richard Boyle, another Englishman, who arrived in Ireland aged 22 with 27 pounds in his pocket and died the country's richest man. Boyle settled in Lismore, enlarged the castle and was later given the title of Earl of Cork. He had fourteen children—seven girls and seven boys—one of whom was the philosopher and scientist, Robert Boyle, who partly financed the printing of the Irish bible I saw at the Bolton Library in Cashel. Another was Cromwell's friend, the horrible Lord Broghill.

We walk through the seventeenth-century riding house, down its wooden staircase and into the lower garden. I remember all the early mornings I used to come here to let the dogs out for a run. Abbey is busy sniffing some bracken while we are walking through the yew walk and doesn't notice a red squirrel prancing across the path. As it's autumn none of the azaleas and camellia bushes are in bloom, but the six Nymans silver trees planted by the duchess 25 years ago below the east wing are a mass of delicate white flowers. It seems a lifetime ago that we used to play croquet in the evenings here on this flat lawn, while chain-smoking my father's Sullivan and Powell Turkish cigarettes in an ineffectual effort to ward off the midges.

Having been around the gardens Louise asks if I would like to go inside the castle. We don't go into the east wing where my family used to live because that is rented out, but look around the main part where the Duke and Duchess of Devonshire and their family reside when they are here.

At the far end of the castle before the huge old kitchen, with its big stone sinks and large well-scrubbed wooden table, is the banqueting hall. For 400 years, between when Prince John built it and Sir Walter Raleigh owned it, the castle was the residence of the bishops of Lismore. And this wood-panelled room with its Gothic-style red and gold walls and star-studded ceiling, designed by Augustus Pugin in the mid-nineteenth century, was originally a medieval chapel. It was in here that we had a big dance the Christmas before my father retired and my parents moved to the cottage. As I reflect on my own memories of time spent in this splendid room, I can also imagine the bishops and their clerics sitting in the choir stalls lining the walls hundreds of years before.

Lord William Burlington, the present Duke of Devonshire's son, is a photographer and in the billiard room is an exquisite collection of black and white photographs he has taken of all the people working on the Lismore Estate. He has also set up a gallery in the west wing which is open to the public and has exhibitions of modern art. Hanging in the wide corridor off the main hall down to the dining room is a series of works on slate by the English artist Richard Long. I discover later the pieces of slate are from the castle roof and the mud with which they are marked is from the Blackwater. Louise also shows me the series of paintings done by David Nash of the yew walk.

In one of the main bedrooms are a series of watercolours depicting the castle before it was renovated 150 years ago by the Sixth Duke of Devonshire who, with the help of his ex-gardener and friend Sir Joseph Paxton, created the castle as it stands today. It was Sir Joseph who designed Crystal Palace for London's Great Exhibition during the reign of Queen Victoria.

We are walking from bedroom to bedroom when Louise stops at a small door I have never noticed before. She unlocks it and leads me up the narrow staircase onto the roof. On one side we look down on the courtyard and across at the gate tower. In the distance I can make out the tall bell tower of St Carthage's Catholic Church in the middle of the town.

It is a clear sunny evening and crossing to the other side of the roof we can also see the familiar purple contours of the Knockmealdown Mountains one way and the wide Blackwater River snaking its way down towards the sea the other. Below on the inches is the stand of silver poplars which was planted a couple of years ago by the estate in memory of my father. He loved trees and had a great interest in forestry. I know he planted hundreds of poplars during his life, and it's very touching that these elegant trees are here in remembrance of him.

It is almost dark by the time I head back to Tourtane. I'm walking on the righthand side of the road, aware that drivers may not see me, but what I hadn't reckoned on was a car overtaking another one from behind me. Suddenly a vehicle going frighteningly fast passes within inches of me. Feeling blessed to be alive I walk the rest of the way back on the verge or in the ditch. I reach Tourtane's gates to be greeted by a large Déise flag fluttering in the breeze. Hopefully, God, the Pope and the Déise are all on the same wavelength.

25

Pre-match fever

I come down to breakfast to find Ambrose, the Triggs' green Amazonian parrot, standing on the kitchen table eating a bowl of muesli. Seeing me he lifts his head, then, stock still, gives me a long disdainful stare. Nick and he have breakfast together every day, and I can tell in the parrot's eyes that I am an unwelcome intruder. Nevertheless, I stand my ground and sit myself at the opposite end of the table, while he jealously commands all Nick's attention. Alison tells me later she always has breakfast in bed because she can't bear watching Ambrose stepping in the butter.

It's pouring with rain, so the perfect day for testing my new '100 per cent waterproof' plastic trousers as I walk the mile and a half back into Lismore. Despite the spray from all the trucks and an elderly man in a small car flying two Déise flags stopping and offering me a lift, I persist with my walk and am delighted to reach town quite dry.

Nick thinks the supposed birthplace of St Declan, which is on the next section of St Declan's Way between here and

Cappoquin, is on land belonging to Michael McGrath, Lismore's butcher. Michael is the third generation of McGraths to run the business and his family have been butchers for 200 years. Michael rears his own lambs and Angus and Hereford cattle. He is one of very few Irish butchers to have his own abattoir, which is at the rear of the shop. So he quite literally provides meat from the field to the plate. Inside the shop legs of lamb and well-aged beef hang from traditional steel racks which run across the ceiling. Three Michaels work at McGraths. Apart from Michael McGrath himself, there is Mikey Whelan, who has worked there for years, and Michael Kearney. Michael McGrath's son, John, also works there. I walk in to find them all decked out in Déise colours. They're wearing white trilby-shaped hats with blue and white checked bands, and blue and white checked aprons. As always Michael McGrath gives me a warm welcome and asks after my mother.

St Declan's birthplace, it transpires, is not on Michael's land, but across the road. The owner of the land has recently died, so rather than worry his widow, Michael suggests I just have a look around. He says babies that died before they were baptised used to be buried there. There is also a grave of a man who drowned in the Blackwater. The bodies of IRA members were laid there during the Troubles, but Michael thinks they were moved later. And he says there is a monument of a ship there, which a man erected in memory of his son who died at sea.

Michael also tells me about St Declan's Well of Toor near Geosh, which he says is good for skin disorders. He had a growth on his neck that the doctor burnt off three times, but it kept growing back. So he went to the well on three consecutive Sundays—'You have to go three times,' he explains—and put water on the growth. It has never returned.

Lismore is in a fever of pre-match excitement. Even the window of Simon Dunn's antique shop has a supportive display of blue and white porcelain, and I see a young boy sitting on the steps of the hairdresser's with a head of blue and white hair. The street where Dan Shanahan, the Déise star player and nominated Hurler of the Year, lives is a mass of flags hanging from windows and bunting running along the roofs and fences. On a telegraph pole is a large handwritten sign saying, 'Good Luck Dan'. Underneath two hurleys frame a large photograph of him.

Pam Stevenson told me that Eamonn, who owns the Eamonn's Place bar, has a framed article hanging up about Petticoat Loose, so I call in to have a look at it. It is no longer on the wall, because Eamonn has just refurbished the place. However, he says he'll have a look for it upstairs, so I order some tea and sit at one of the lounge seats.

Five minutes later a bevy of librarians from University College Cork comes through the door, order tea and coffee, and sit themselves down around me. They have just been on a tour of the castle and its gardens, and also visited the cathedral library. When I ask the librarians which side they reckon will win the All-Ireland on Sunday, I'm told that Waterford are 'grasping at straws' thinking they are likely to beat Kilkenny.

Eamonn is unable to find the piece on Petticoat Loose. I finish my tea and leave, thinking maybe these librarians are a little sour because the Cork team are not in the final, as they are usually hot contenders to win the series.

My mother Marabella often used to send me up New Street, where I'm walking now, to get cream from Mrs Casey who lived here and did the milk run in town. The low terraced cottages along the street were built by the Sixth Duke of Devonshire nearly 200 years ago, when he relocated all the people living by the castle walls. They were so indignant about the forced move that they claimed they had been sent to Botany Bay—the penal colony in Sydney—and to this day the street is still referred to as Botany.

Further on is the old train station, where King Edward VII and Queen Alexandra arrived 100 years ago when they came to stay with the Duke and Duchess of Devonshire at the castle. Beyond is what once was the workhouse, a large stone building with an overgrown garden that now stands empty.

Workhouses were built all around Ireland several years before the Great Famine of 1845–1852 in response to the huge increase in the country's population and the number of people living in poverty. In those days no relief was given to anyone outside the workhouses. To be eligible for admission people had to relinquish any land or property they owned. Inside the regime was severe. Families were split up and men, women and children had separate areas. The inmates made their own clothes and grew their own food and worked, and there was little contact with the outside world.

The Lismore workhouse had accommodation for 500 people. But a couple of years after it was built, it was contending with the famine. At one stage there were 700 inmates, most of whom were starving and disease ridden. They had to endure life in a building with overflowing stinking lavatories and rain coming through its walls.

There were so many deaths during the famine both inside and out of the workhouse, especially from typhus and relapsing fever, that the Duke of Devonshire gave the Catholic Church 2 acres of land on Chapel Street for victims to be buried. Walking down the road into this huge walled area I wonder just how many people died to warrant such a large burial ground. Later I read that a reporter from the *Cork Examiner* was sent to Lismore to report on the effect of the famine. He saw a pit being opened in the newly acquired graveyard, where 40 bodies had been interred in one week alone.

Before leaving Lismore and heading back to the Triggs I call in to see Ann McCarthy at the Wine Vaults. She's standing at the till, and on a table near the window are the homemade breads and cakes she baked earlier in the day.

The Wine Vaults not only has a good selection of wines, but is also a large grocery store, which since Florence, her husband, died she has run on her own with some help from her children and a few staff.

The town is quieter than usual for a Friday afternoon and the boy, who assists Ann in the afternoons after school, tells me many people have already left for Dublin for the game.

'I'm going on Sunday, myself,' he adds proudly.

I arrive back at Tourtane to find Nick and Alison debating who will look after Ambrose if they die. Not only can Amazonian green parrots live up to 70 years, but they also have memories like elephants and Nick and Alison's sons, Charles and James, in their youth both did something reprehensible in Ambrose's eyes, so are not tolerated, and so did Harvey, Nick and Alison's eldest grandson. Baz, their ten-year-old second grandson, they conclude, may be the only person not to have blotted his copy book with this unforgiving bird.

26

A cloistered existence

The sky is clear this morning and there's not a hint of
rain. Having previously arranged with Sister Agnes
via email to be at St Mary's Abbey for lunch, I set off
mid-morning, walking initially along the main road towards
Tallow then down a quiet back road to Glencairn. I pass Dick
Nugent's garage, which has a notice pinned to the door, saying,
'Closed Monday 8 September due to All-Ireland Sickness'.

As I walk down the drive to St Mary's Abbey a herd of
bullocks raise their heads from the lush green grass and stare
at me. A large oak tree partly obscures the abbey itself and
the adjoining buildings of the convent. As a family we came
here several times for services, but apart from the interior of
the church I have little memory of the place.

There is no answer when I press the front door bell, so I
go around to the side of the building and ring another bell
there. Five minutes later a nun appears from behind me. She
is wearing a dark blue padded sleeveless jacket over her habit

and her short grey hair sticks out from under her black veil. She introduces herself as Sister Kathleen and opens the door, which is the entrance to the guesthouse, then takes me upstairs to my room. Sister Kathleen suggests I spend some time settling in before coming down to lunch at half past twelve.

My room is called St Anne, after the mother of the Virgin Mary. There is a large statue of her in the corner. Above the single bed against the wall is a crucifix. There is a small wash basin and next to it a small pine wardrobe and a chest of drawers. At the end of the room, an armchair is placed in front of a low window that looks out onto the courtyard below.

A timetable has been left on the narrow table opposite the bed. At 3 p.m. is None and Vespers at 6 p.m. This is followed by Benediction at 7.45 p.m. and Compline at 7.55 p.m. Then tomorrow morning is Vigils at 4.10 a.m., Lauds at 7.45 a.m., Terce 8.45 a.m. and Mass at 11 a.m. As I read all the services, I wonder what I have let myself in for.

Four places are laid at one of the long refectory tables in the dining room, but there is no sign of the three other guests who are staying, so I walk across the courtyard to the church. The interior of the church is surprisingly modern. There are no pews, instead upright chairs line the walls. A plump lady wearing a navy skirt and cardigan is praying in the visitor's section at the back. I also notice a nun sitting in the choir stalls above the square white altar. I sit for a moment, just taking in my surroundings, then quietly tiptoe out again.

Back in the dining room I meet Gemma. Although she is wearing everyday clothes, Gemma is a Sister of Our Lady of Charity. Based in Dublin she works with prostitutes and trafficked women who have been bought from overseas for sexual exploitation. She and her friend Lorraine have been here a week and are leaving today.

It turns out that Carmel, who was praying in the church, is also a nun, a member of the French Sisters of Charity of St Vincent de Paul, which she joined 33 years ago at the age of eighteen. She has been a school chaplain in Cork teaching deprived children, but is about to go to Chicago for a year. She is round and bubbly and funny, and, sadly for me, is also leaving today.

They have all heard I am on a pilgrimage, presumably from Sister Agnes, and ask why I decided to do it. I tell them about my previous pilgrimage to Santiago de Compostela in Spain. Then I explain how much I love the walking, being able to amble along eating blackberries, and also the joy of seeing the trees and the wildflowers.

Lunch is oxtail soup followed by lamb, baked potatoes, chips, a warm grated carrot dish and mushy peas, and then apple pie and custard. It isn't until we have eaten that I learn all the nuns are actually vegetarian, and eat meat only if they sick or need a 'pick-me-up'.

After we wash up Sister Agnes and Sister Kathleen appear to see the others off. Sister Agnes is 78 years old. She has white hair and rosy cheeks and a beautiful serenity about her. She has been here at St Mary's for 50 years and has done a couple of six-year stints as abbess. She is currently the prioress. Although this week she is acting abbess, as the abbess and two other nuns have gone to Italy for a Cistercian general chapter meeting. Sister Agnes is originally from Kilkenny, but she says she wants Waterford to win the match tomorrow.

I stand with the two nuns and wave off Lorraine, Gemma and Carmel. Then Sister Kathleen disappears to 'steal a pair of gumboots' for me, so that I can take Barney, the convent's old collie, for a walk down to the river. I'm not sure whether the 3 p.m. None is not happening, or if the nuns do not think I should attend, but they tell me the next call to prayer is Vespers at 6 p.m.

Barney and I walk around a field of recently cut wheat and along beside the Blackwater. The river is wide and fast from the rain and runs through the trailing leaves of an ash tree growing on its bank. A startled heron flies up into a tree as we approach. The old Irish name for this land is *Ballingrane*, which means 'the townsland of the horse'. Only 3 miles upstream from Lismore it was originally part of the Lismore monastic settlement.

The path turns away from the river and goes through the woods. Beeches, sycamores and horse chestnuts form a thick canopy. The woodland floor is a carpet of green except for the occasional head of orangey-red berries of a single stem of lords and ladies poking up through the undergrowth. The path cuts through a covering of ivy before reaching a shallow stream with a bed of red stones. The water quietly tinkles and gently shakes the sycamore leaves which are floating in it.

I turn back and Barney flushes a cock pheasant out of the Himalayan balsam as we reach the Blackwater again. The sun pierces the grey clouds throwing its light onto the small white feathers clinging to a couple of wheat stalks and an elder dripping with its dark berries. A rabbit darts across the field. I watch bees as they crawl into the pink lips of the Himalayan balsam.

As I walk I think about a question I was asked at lunch: do I call myself a pilgrim? I'm not bursting with religious zeal or walking to a destination in the hope of reaching nirvana. But I do hope that I'll experience some sort of transformation. Interestingly, the word 'pilgrim' comes from the Latin *per agrum*, meaning 'through the fields'. Perhaps this journey is just that, a walk along narrow roads, across mountains and through fields. Though it has a purpose, it is not about the destination, but rather about connecting with the sacred in its many forms along the way. I love walking through the land, and the joy of seeing the trees, the moss and the flowers nourishes me in some way and gives me a strong sense of being part of everything around me.

I'm back in the dining room at 5.15 p.m. for supper and although Sister Agnes said two other guests are here this evening, neither appear. A nun wearing a white veil comes in with some pasta. Her name is Denise, and she is a New Yorker. Before she came here she spent 32 years with the Missionaries of Charity, a contemplative branch of an order established by Mother Teresa of Calcutta. Denise has been at Glencairn for about a year and likes being in a closed order, because the nuns spend lots of time alone and are not going out into the world. 'I'm so happy here,' she says, 'it is everything I always dreamt of.' She has not yet taken her final vows, which is why she is wearing a white veil rather than a black one. Although she must be 50, she has a very clear unlined face and exudes a youthful innocence.

On my way back to my room I meet Eithne (pronounced Etna), one of the other guests. Originally from Dublin and now living in Canada, Eithne is thin and wiry with a tanned face full of wrinkles and a well-cut bob of grey hair. The polo neck jumper and slacks she is wearing give her quite a young appearance, but I suspect Eithne is elderly, and I quickly discover also quite deaf.

The third guest Josephine is also elderly. Her skin is so pale it is almost blue. Josephine is from Holy Cross near Cashel, and comes here every year. Sisters Agnes and Denise flutter around her and when she says she does not want pasta for supper, Denise hurries away to make her a quiche.

At Vespers I notice four other nuns in the church wearing white veils, one looks Indian, another African. I wonder what it must be like for them living in rural Ireland in an enclosed community with a lot of elderly nuns. All the nuns tunics are white, over which they wear a black scapular with a belt round their waists, similar to the garb of the Cistercian monks at Mount Melleray. Some very old nuns sit near the visitors' area at the back of the church, but the rest are singing psalms in the choir stalls. Every so often a single voice sings a line then the rest join in. They are not trained voices, but mellow from years of practice.

Eithne, Josephine and I go together from the guesthouse to the church for Benediction at 7.45 p.m. 'Beautiful evening,' Eithne remarks as we step out into the open air. Starlings circle above us. 'Beautiful evening,' Eithne reiterates, just as we are entering the church. A few nuns are already there, sitting in silence, which is instantly broken by Eithne asking me very loudly what psalms are going to be sung and Josephine stamping her feet on the floor. I watch the nuns glide serenely into the choir stalls, and instantly wish I was up there with them rather than down this end with the bellowing and the stamping.

The nuns sing a hymn about the end of the day and the evening light highlights the purple and lilac panes of the stained-glass windows. After the Lord's Prayer the nuns file out through a side door and the three of us walk out through the back door into the courtyard. 'Beautiful evening,' says Eithne, looking up at the half moon hovering below the branches of a tree. Josephine walks ahead and then exclaims that her key does not open the door of the guesthouse. I go to help and discover she is putting it into the lock upside-down. 'Beautiful evening,' booms Eithne into the night.

27

Dawn chorus

The bell rings. It is dark and cold. I quickly dress and head across to the church. The sky is full of stars and it feels like the middle of the night to me, but for the nuns it is a start of a new day. Vigils, the 4.10 a.m. session, is obviously for the young and brave. The elderly nuns are not there and neither are Eithne and Josephine. I have to admit once it is over I hop back into bed for a while before getting up again to do yoga.

At quarter to eight the bell goes for Lauds. I wish I could join in the singing of the psalms and the canticles, but as I do not know the melody I stand and listen, as the different solo voices sing a line followed by the others. Terce, an hour later, follows hot on its heels. Rays of sun stream through the stained-glass windows as the nuns sing their psalms praising and giving thanks to God.

Josephine appears in the dining room while I'm having breakfast, and I ask if she slept well.

'I haven't slept at all,' she replies crossly, as she sprinkles four spoons of sugar onto her cornflakes. Eithne appears shortly afterwards and stands at the sideboard peeling an orange and then cuts herself two door stops of bread, which get stuck in the toaster.

While we are clearing up breakfast Josephine tells me she loves the nuns here because they are so happy. The monks at Mount Saint Joseph in Tipperary, near where she comes from, she says, are not very happy because they have so many worries. I adore the nuns, too, but I wonder if it is because we are women. The atmosphere here at Glencairn to me is quite different to Mount Melleray, which felt like a bit of a boys' club.

I have been given an introduction by a friend to a Sister Gertrude who asks me to come and see her at ten o'clock. Sister Gertrude is sitting on a wooden chair in a sparsely furnished room off the main entrance. She tells me St Mary's Abbey was founded 80 years ago and when she first came here 45 years ago some of the original founders were still alive. In those days all the food they ate, except for sugar, they produced themselves. They grew all their own vegetables and made their own bread. They kept chickens for eggs, and also had a dairy, so had their own milk, butter and cream.

As an enclosed order the nuns did not go out, so the doctor and the dentist, as well as an optician and a man selling shoes, would come here. Also Mount Melleray provided a chaplain who did any shopping they needed. But today, Sister Gertrude says, they have to go out. Mount Melleray's dwindling numbers mean that a monk can no longer be spared to be a chaplain.

The doctor does still visit on a regular basis, but if a nun is ill in between visits they have to take her to the doctor. She adds that last night one of the nuns drove to Fermoy to collect Josephine from the bus. They are more enclosed than the monks at Mount Melleray, she says, who for various reasons, such as the school, always have had to go out more.

Sister Gertrude milked the cows for seventeen years, but the abbey no longer has a dairy herd. The European Union laws have made the logistics too difficult, she explains. Instead the nuns keep cattle and also make greeting cards and communion wafers, which are sold all over the world. She looks after the woodlands and tells me, as this is the wettest summer in Ireland for the last 150 years, that the Himalayan balsam and rushes are growing in places where they have never grown before.

Because this is a silent order, Sister Gertrude explains, among themselves the nuns do not talk, unless it is absolutely necessary, and in which case the matter is quietly discussed. However, hospitality has always been an important part of their mission, so they can talk to visitors. I blush at the thought of all the questions with which I have bombarded Sister Agnes and Sister Denise, and how they never once appeared unhappy to talk. And now I can't help quizzing Sister Gertrude!

I ask if she thinks her time here has changed her. Like when I have spoken to the other sisters, she answers very openly and directly. She says it is hard to see herself, but she has noticed changes in other people. Nuns with difficult temperaments who were hard to get on with have softened.

'I've seen the working of grace,' she concludes.

Our conversation ends when a couple from Slovakia start to take photographs at the front door with some of the nuns, and Sister Gertrude goes off to get her camera.

'Come on, Gertie,' cries Sister Kathleen, as we all stand in front of the door, 'take the photograph.'

The nuns giggle and laugh as they decide who should be in the next shot, and it is hard to imagine that most of their time together is spent in silence. Then Sister Agnes appears and my photograph is taken with her, before the nuns all scurry away to get ready for Mass at eleven o'clock.

So many visitors come to this Sunday Mass that we do not all fit in the visitors' section of the church, and some people sit with the nuns. Elderly nuns who have not been present at other prayer sessions, because Sister Agnes says they have been unwell, appear, and I count 28 nuns in total.

Most of the nuns wear a cream-coloured cowl over their habits which has wide sleeves that are so long they come down to their shins, so as one walks up to the lectern to read a lesson she really does look like a sort of penguin. Then with incredible deftness she pushes these long sleeves up and her hands appear and turn the pages of the huge bible.

The visitors as well as the nuns sing this morning, much to my delight after sitting at every prayer session and wishing I could join in. Prayers are said including one for the safety of all the people travelling to Dublin today to watch the All-Ireland game.

I leave straight after Mass, and, as I kiss Josephine goodbye, realise I have grown fond of my two eccentric co-guests. Eithne says she'll come with me up the drive. As we walk she tells me when she was growing up in Dublin only two houses in her street owned a car. We are striding along extolling the benefits of walking when a man stops his car to offer us a lift. I stoutly refuse but look longingly at the little vehicle which could have carried my backpack and me at least some of the way back to Tourtane.

I feel touched by my time with the nuns at St Mary's Abbey. Their devotion is powerful, and their directness and openness is beautiful. With all the nuns I spoke to, I never once felt that information was being withheld and yet nothing any of them said was irrelevant. As an enclosed order they are not out feeding the poor and nursing the sick, instead their days are spent mostly in prayer. At each of the prayer sessions in the 24 hours I was there, the light through the stained-glass windows at the top of the church was different, and as the nuns sang the psalms and the canticles praising God and all his creation, it was a beautiful reminder of the presence of the divine in everything and each moment.

28

Déise disaster

James, Nick and Alison's second son, and his black labrador, Shelper, are at Tourtane when I arrive. James has worked with horses all his adult life and now runs a successful horse dentistry practice. He has lived and worked in England and America, as well as other parts of Ireland, but like me he adores the Déise.

James is in the process of buying 23 acres of land on the far side of the Lismore woods, and he drives me up to see it. We pull up beside some farm buildings which he will own and walk down to what he says is a castle. When I remark that this ruin is the smallest castle I have ever seen, as it is only one room, and looks to me more like a tower, he replies that he is only small, too.

The land slopes down towards the Bride River. Old Tom Morgan, who lives near here, told me that only 60 years ago he used to see a two-masted sailing boat bringing coal up the Bride to Tallow, and return with corn. On the other side of the river, halfway up the hill, is the little Fountain Church where my father is buried.

'Don't worry,' says James, gazing across the valley, 'I'll keep an eye on Paul.'

As we stand on the hillside in a field of clover looking down at the river, James tells me he will find a four-leaf clover here. I immediately scan around me, looking for one of those elusive good luck tokens, but then I remember, for its powers to work, it must be found by chance and not by actively searching. The four leaves represent faith, hope, love and luck. It's believed that the significance of the four-leaf clover pre-dates Christianity, and that it was a Celtic charm regarded as having potent powers over bad spirits. Apparently, the possessor of one will not only have great luck, but also be able to see fairies. They are said to grow where a mare has been born or dropped her first foal, which, given that James's life and work revolves around horses, is probably why he finds them and I don't.

Listening to James's plans to build a house here, I am filled with excitement at how he must feel to finally have his piece of land in this pocket of Ireland, where he was born and has always returned to over the years. He belongs to this land, and although I have made my life with Stephen thousands of miles away, I realise that part of me will always belong to this land, too, which is one reason why I'm here now, walking St Declan's Way.

Alison has roasted a piece of Michael McGrath's beef for Sunday lunch and for pudding we have raspberries from the garden. Then the rest of the Trigg family settles in front of the television to watch the match. But, because my mother Marabella is arriving back from her stay in England with my uncle, Alison and I drive to Cork to collect her from the airport.

We listen to the game on the car radio. In the first minute the Kilkenny Cats get a point, but ten seconds later Waterford score so they are even. For the next few minutes there is high-speed commentary before Kilkenny gains one point, quickly followed by another. Waterford scores, but shortly afterwards Kilkenny pulls ahead again, and its 5 to 2, then 6 to 2, before Eoin Kelly, who seems to be the only one of the Déise making a difference to the game, scores a point bringing it up to 3 for Waterford.

In the next ten minutes Eoin Kelly gets one more point and then the Cats' points climb up to 10 before they confirm their lead with a goal, which is quickly followed by another goal, putting them well ahead with two goals and 10 points to Waterford's measly 4 points. A couple of times Lismore's hero, Dan Shanahan, gets the ball but it comes to nothing, and only Eoin Kelly manages to score one more point to Kilkenny's additional 6 before half time.

Alison and I are no hurling buffs, but even we realise as we pull up at the airport that the Déise have been well and truly squashed. And an hour and half later when we arrive back at Tourtane the Déise flag has already been removed by Charles from the front gate.

29

Battling the undergrowth

It's Monday morning, and I linger for the last time at the Triggs' kitchen table. Then, half the morning gone as usual, I set off with my backpack down the drive, and into Lismore to rejoin St Declan's Way. Nick's parting words are that he has just received an email from a friend in America and apparently the vestiges of Hurricane Hanna are whirling across the Atlantic and due in Ireland tomorrow, which means torrential rain.

I'm not unduly worried about time as I have only about 7 miles to cover today. The elderly man in the small car sporting the Déise flags stops again, and, not feeling the need to walk along this busy main road yet another time, I accept a lift into Lismore. Wistfully he tells me he didn't expect Waterford to win against Kilkenny, but never thought they would do as badly as they did. The score at the end of the match was 3–30 to 1–13, and Waterford's only goal was actually a Kilkenny home one. The contribution from the Lismore boys was one miserable point from Dan Shanahan and one from Dave Bennett. Admittedly, Kilkenny has been trying to win four All-Irelands in a row for more than 70 years and yesterday finally succeeded, but for a Waterford person that is hardly the issue.

The old man drops me off at the monument and I walk towards the bridge. On the lefthand side of the road water gushes out from a gap in the high outer wall of the castle into a large moss-covered stone basin. Known as the Spout, its water comes from a natural spring. The water is known for its healing properties and often I have seen people filling bottles with it, although the Spout is equally popular as a car wash.

I remember that Kieran Heffernan told me in medieval times before pilgrims departed from Lismore along the Way they used to visit the anchorite, a monk who had voluntarily agreed to be walled up for life in a tiny cell in order to spend his time in prayer away from the distractions of the world. At the ruined Okyle Church between here and Camphire, the remains of the anchor cell can still be seen. It is less than 6 feet long and 5 feet wide, symbolising a grave. The monk entered it through a doorway which was subsequently bricked up, and a funeral service was given as recognition that the anchorite was dead to the world. From then on food and water were given to him through a small opening into the interior of the church, and through another small slot he gave counsel and spiritual advice to the outside world. Records show there have been at least seven known anchorites at Lismore and apparently the townland of Ballyanchor was the anchorite's endowment, giving him an income for food and clothes.

With no such adviser today I fill my bottle with water from the Spout and pass through the iron kissing gate and onto the path that runs alongside the Blackwater, known as Lady Louisa's Walk, which is also the route of St Declan's Way. In the woodlands on the embankment above the river my presence disturbs a little egret. Due to climate change in the past 25 years, these dazzling white birds have taken up residence on the Blackwater.

Further on the path runs through a field next to the river where a couple of men are fly-fishing. Ahead is the Round Hill, where I am heading, crowned by a stand of tall Scots pines. A cormorant flies across the water to a small island. I jump over a little stream and follow an indistinct path, which becomes narrower and narrower. The Himalayan balsam growing either side of it becomes increasingly taller until it towers above my head. A robin flits in front of me, perching for a moment on a stem of a leaf with its tail quivering.

Emerging from the balsam I face a field full of nettles. Thinking a scythe would be useful at this point, I remember the dream my landlady had about me walking St Declan's Way before I left home. She saw me hacking my way through the Irish undergrowth with a pair of shears.

I turn back, leave the bank of the river and head into the woodlands where I immediately find a path. But after a while the path fades out, so I retrace my steps and walk along the side of a field. I clamber under a couple of electric fences and then over a few barbed wire ones before finding myself unable to keep going due to insurmountable brambles. So I turn back again, ignore a sign which says, 'Danger Quarry', and find a new path.

Every time I have walked along here to the Round Hill it hasn't been straightforward. Whether it is because I have lost my way so many times I have no memory of the right way, or because the path is very unclear, I'll never know. At one point I'm back beside the river and find growing in the watery ground young white willows with their long narrow greyish leaves. It is said the willow is sacred to the Celtic moon goddess because it is the tree that loves water most, and the moon goddess presides over water.

Going around the quarry, I eventually arrive at what was once an Iron Age fort, the Round Hill. Ravens circle above the green heads of the long elegant Scots pines growing on top of it. I decide against even attempting to climb the hill today as all efforts to do so in the past have proved futile. Maybe the *aes sídhe*, the mound fairies, have made it impenetrable. Ragwort, which is growing in abundance here, is believed to be ridden, like a horse, by fairies, so maybe they are the only ones with access, as they fly up there on this toxic yellow weed.

At the Round Hill the Way of Patrick's Cow deviates off in a different direction to St Declan's Way. I continue on *Bóthar na Naomh*, the Road of the Saints, the name by which this section of the Way is known.

Michael McGrath told me that the reputed birthplace of St Declan was next to a disused farmyard along this road, so when I reach a farmyard next to a large yew tree I assume I'm in the right place. An old stone cottage with a rusty corrugated iron roof stands derelict in the overgrown yard, and the area around the yew tree is covered with nettles. Using a long piece of wood I find in the barn, I start to hack my way through the nettles. Michael said there was a monument of a ship, but despite my rigorous thrashing I can see nothing. Eventually, I decide it can not be as inaccessible as this, so give up and continue down the road. I feel mortified by the nettle demolition job I have just done in the farmyard and can only hope the owners find my clearing effort useful.

A bit further along a grey-haired woman is turning her car and when I ask her for directions she tells me to go to the next gate. I find the old iron gate, climb over it and walk across the field to a clump of trees enclosed by a wire fence. Covered in ivy is a stone edifice which has a V-shaped archway, the top of which tails down to the ground, so it looks a bit like a large stone tent. I learn later this is the Honan Cenotaph which was erected by Sir William Honan in memory of his son who was lost at sea. Brambles are growing all around it, so I pick up a stick and start to bash through them until I am close enough to see a large stone cross. On it is inscribed the date 1821 and the words:

> Death dwells here in silence
> No tombs record the grief of parents.
> Here are no monuments of parents themselves
> Nothing to proclaim the vanity of grieving
> for those whom we so soon must follow.

On a headstone is a Latin poem about the brevity of life, and underneath the poem what looks initially like a skull and cross bones turns out, on closer inspection, to be a profile of a child's head. I think of the unbaptised babies buried here and the parents grieving for the short lives of their offspring, who for no fault of their own were not allowed to be buried on consecrated ground. It is a gloomy place. I had hoped that St Declan's birthplace would be special, and not this sad, overgrown, forgotten place. After all, not only is he a saint, but he is also believed to be a descendent of the Kings of Tara who presided over all of Ireland. When he was born people in the neighbourhood saw a ball of fire on the roof of the house where he lay. It reached up to heaven, was surrounded by a multitude of angels and assumed the shape of a ladder.

As I leave the depressingly neglected spot I wonder if the Déise would have done better in the match yesterday if they had made a bit more effort with their own patron saint, instead of going for the support of the Pope.

30

Detour to Tourin

Finches fly in and out of the hedgerows and a rabbit hops onto the road before seeing me and disappearing into the ditch. A mile later I turn off the Road of the Saints and walk up to Tourin House.

When I spoke to my friend Kristin Jameson this morning I said I would be with her by one o'clock. She casually said she would take something out of the fridge for lunch, so I'm not unduly worried that it is now ten to two. But I arrive to discover Kristin and her sister, Tara, sitting in the little dining room. They have now nearly finished a three-course lunch with the County Waterford manager, Ray O'Dwyer and his two children, Ashling and Hugh, who are not at school today because it is closed due to the match.

Kristin tells me later that the O'Dwyers were sitting next to the President of Ireland, Mary McAleese, at Croke Park yesterday. Young Hugh gives an entertaining account of the anticipation of the crowd prior to the match, and the outfits and shenanigans of various Déise supporters, followed by their steady exodus after the first few minutes of the game when they realised that Waterford was being pummelled into the ground. Meanwhile, Ray explains that the two homecoming celebrations planned for the team have been cut to just one.

I was very much in awe of the three Jameson sisters when I was young. They were always at the many West Waterford drinks parties and to me they all seemed very creative and elusive. Following in the footsteps of their grandmother, the painter Joan Jameson, Kristin and Andrea were artists, and Tara decorated porcelain. Their mother, Didi, was Norwegian and met Shane, their father, on Norway's only golf course shortly after the war. When they got married she came to live in this grand Italianate-style house in West Waterford, bringing with her a Norwegian rowing boat and two wood-burning stoves.

Kristin takes me to look at the ruined 350-year-old Tourin Castle. Ivy grows up the walls and winds its way around the windows. According to Irish folklore the elder tree once refused to shelter Christ, but the ivy gave him shelter, and this is why the elder is the last tree to come into leaf in spring and why ivy is evergreen. Ivy is extremely strong and difficult to destroy. Although it has its roots in the ground, it uses other trees or structures to climb quickly off the ground and up towards the light, so is believed to symbolise the soul and its journey and search for nourishment.

From the castle we walk down to the old stone quay on the Blackwater. Tourin, Kristin tells me, means a bleaching green in Irish, and flax was grown here and left in the low bogland area we are looking at to bleach. As we stand on this still afternoon watching the swollen brown river slide silently past, it is hard to imagine that 400 years ago, due to the entrepreneurism of the First Earl of Cork and all his industries, that this waterway would have been buzzing with activity. And that less than 70 years ago trading vessels still stopped here, as well as at Cappoquin, with cargoes of coal, and on their return journey down the river to Youghal carried iron ore, linen and pit props.

Further along the river Kristin points out some spires, the rushes used for thatching. Upstream of them she indicates another low-lying area. 'There used to be reedy bogs here,' she says, 'but my father drained them, and my grandfather wouldn't talk to him for going on a year because he had destroyed the snipe shooting.' Kristin has just planted 70 acres of this area with native Sissile oak, the oak that used to grow here, and a few other hardwoods including chestnut and cherry.

'When my father was a child there used to be twelve gardeners,' recounts Kristin, as we look around the walled garden. 'Goodness knows how many glasshouses there were,' she continues. 'There was the grape house and a peach house, a tomato house and then there was the chrysanthemum and arum lily house. The greenhouses used to be centrally heated. There was a boiler room and the boiler was fuelled by coal, and had to be kept stoked day and night.'

We walk into a remaining glasshouse in which tomatoes and geraniums are growing. 'Look,' says Kristin, pointing excitedly to a patch of dry soil, 'this is where the partridges dust. Because it's so wet outside they've found their way in here.' Dusting is the partridges' way of getting of rid of lice, she explains. They dig themselves down in the dirt then flap their wings and the dry earth rubs off the lice, which they promptly eat, so they get a protein fix as well.

'We pretty much grow all our own vegetables,' says Kristin, pulling out some weeds along the path between the raised beds of the walled garden. 'We sell our plums and also the cherries.' At one time there were three generations of the family living in the house, she recounts, as well as a number of aunts and cousins. The kitchen garden and farm produced enough food to make them self-sufficient, which was especially important during the two World Wars.

When Kristin was growing up she remembers that anyone working at, or connected to, Tourin was offered a drill of potatoes. Some were in the kitchen garden and some in a field. Not everyone took up the drill, but many people did, and it meant they had potatoes for their family. 'The harvest took a couple of days,' she says. 'The potatoes were first dug up then picked up off the ground. Andrea, Tara and I and all the other children helped.'

In this garden Tara also grows all the flowers for the flower-arranging business she now has, including more than 100 different types of irises. I can imagine the flowers make a great splash of colour in the summer, but now in the first throes of autumn most have died away.

As we walk into the stableyard Kristin points out Andrea's studio, and says that her sister is currently showing an exhibition of her paintings in Newfoundland in Canada, where apparently 75 per cent of the large Irish population can today trace their ancestors back to Waterford.

'Would you like an apple?' Kristin asks. 'I think they might be slightly unripe, but they're still all right.' She picks one off a nearby tree and hands it to me. It has that crispness and slightly sharpish taste of an apple not quite ripe, but tastes delicious.

Heading back to the house we pass Tara and a couple she is showing around the house and gardens, which are open to the public by appointment over the summer months. It starts to rain so we dash indoors, and Kristin takes me past the impressive oak double staircase in the main hall and into her office.

Hanging on the walls are paintings she did when she lived in Italy and Norway. But at the moment she has put her paintbrush aside, and with fortitude and humour is focusing her energies on managing Tourin. I imagine it isn't easy maintaining a large old house and ensuring its land brings in an adequate source of income and I admire her for what she is doing.

She points out another picture on the wall, painted by Joan Jameson of a couple of people thrashing corn. 'It's here in the farmyard,' Kristin explains, 'in around the 1920s.' Then she adds in a definite tone, 'Now tea.'

Tara joins us in the drawing room. The Norwegian wood-burning stove is going and from the window in the grey light the ruined Tourin Castle can be seen across the field. As we flick through wildflower and tree books, identifying some of the plants I have seen on my travels, I realise I'm still in awe of these talented sisters, with their strong connection to their family home and land.

31

Decked out for a dinner party

There have been spasmodic spates of rain all day, but as soon as I set off to walk the couple of miles into Cappoquin, it starts to rain continually, requiring full wet weather regalia.

The road does a 90-degree turn and for a moment I'm once again on the Road of the Saints. I shall be back here tomorrow, because I'm staying with the Martins who live further along it at Drumroe. This evening, though, I'm spending the night with old friends David and Juju Keane in Cappoquin.

The Keanes were originally part of the O'Cahan clan of Derry in the north of Ireland. The O'Cahans fought the English in the Nine Years War at the end of Elizabeth I's reign. They also fought for King James II against King William of Orange at the Battle of the Boyne nearly a century later. After that defeat the O'Cahans' lands in Derry were confiscated and, as they were Catholic, they were also severely restricted by the Penal Laws. Catholics could not stand for parliament, vote, join the army or navy, practise at the bar, buy land or carry a sword. And at any time a Protestant was entitled to pay 5 pounds to a Catholic for his horse and leave him to walk.

Practising Catholicism was not banned, but all church buildings now belonged the Protestant Church of Ireland. This forced the Catholics to celebrate mass on makeshift altar tables such as the one at *Tobar Iosa* in Cahir. Given this state of affairs, David's ancestor Seoirse O'Cahan changed religion, took up law, adopted an anglicised version of his name and became George Keane.

As I approach the small town of Cappoquin I pass a man fly-fishing on the corner where the Blackwater dramatically changes its direction and, having flowed eastwards since it rose in the west of Ireland, here makes a righthand turn and runs south down to the sea. High above the river is the disused iron railway bridge, the construction of which Barbara's great-great-aunt's sweetheart was working on before he committed suicide at Bay Lough.

I cross the bridge and look down at the Cappoquin Boathouse, the home to the town's rowing club. When I worked at the Gate Theatre in Dublin in my twenties, the older actors used to tell me about the plays they performed here, when Michail Mác Liammóir and Hilton Edwards, the founders of the Gate Theatre, toured their productions. Inevitably, during the course of the evening at least one actor would make an impressive exit from the stage and fall into the river.

The rain is still bucketing down as I walk past the low-terraced cottages along Mass Lane and arrive on the doorstep of Tivoli House. The door is opened by David, who takes one look at me in my rainwear and immediately dissolves into laughter. He then says he wants to leave me standing in the rain and go and get his camera.

At that moment Juju appears and exclaims, 'It's Good Fairy Good!' When David and Juju's children were young I played Good Fairy Good in a children's program called *Fortycoats*. I was a fairy with an extremely positive outlook on life. I'd pirouette about happily, always smiling and waving my wand, greeting flowers and trees. But this blissful existence was short-lived, because I was ambushed by the wicked Whirlygig Witch, who locked me up, stole my clothes and pretended to be me. However, when I was eventually rescued by Fortycoats, I still had my unerring optimism and told him, 'I am sure the Whirlygig Witch meant well when she stripped me naked and hung me upside-down in the cupboard.'

When we had finished rehearsals and were about to start filming, one of the regular actors on the series told me, because the program was low budget, the director often would say a scene was fine rather than reshoot it, just to get it in the can. 'If you really stuff up,' she told me, 'just say "fuck", because then they have to cut, as that can't go to air on children's television.' In the end I didn't have to resort to swearing, but the couple of times I had a moment's blank and couldn't remember my lines, 'fuck' was the only word on the tip of my tongue.

David's photo opportunity is spoilt when Juju takes me into the house. During dinner David tells me that Christopher Horsman, who I spoke to on the telephone before I set out, stayed one night at Tivoli when he was walking St Declan's

Way. The following day David walked with him from here to Ardfinnan. Christopher completed St Declan's Way in three days, he recounts. He walked very fast and the only thing that slowed him down were nettles, as he wore shorts. It's a far cry from my slow circuitous peregrinations and I can't imagine going at such a rapid pace.

Christopher walked St Declan's Way fifteen years ago. The map I'm following hadn't been printed and not a single brown metal signpost had been put up, so he found his way using a compass, ordnance survey maps, and from the descriptions and maps in a paper written 100 years ago by Reverend P Power, a man who did a great deal of research into both St Declan and the Way.

Wisely, Christopher did not lug a backpack. He carried a scallop shell which he used to scoop up water to drink from springs and streams, and over his shorts he wore a Barbour jacket. In his pockets he had a flannel and a toothbrush, a spare shirt, two pairs of socks and some disposable paper pants. He also carried a pair of women's black tights. According to David he was inspired by the Frenchman, Chevalier De La Tocnaye, who walked around Ireland 200 years ago carrying a pair of silk stockings and a piece of white chalk to powder his hair, so he was perfectly dressed for dinner with the Marquis of Waterford. When faced with a dinner party Christopher put on the black tights under his shorts, donned the clean shirt, and claimed that this transformed him into an Elizabethan gentleman in a doublet and hose.

32

Sir Richard Keane and the pact with the devil

After breakfast I go through the gate in the wall beside Tivoli House and walk up through the apple orchard to Cappoquin House, the large Georgian building on the hill above the town. This is where David's father, Sir Richard Keane, lives. I pass an orchard of bright green Bramleys, and in what used to be the West Meadow are smaller trees covered in red apples, which Juju tells me later are Worcester Pearmains. There is a stack of wooden boxes in the courtyard in preparation for the picking. Orchards in ancient Ireland were considered sacred places. In Celtic mythology the apple is associated with plenty and abundance, and also with choice and the necessity of making a choice.

I go in through the back door of Cappoquin House and find Anne Ekers, who cooks for Sir Richard, talking to her brother Paul Murray. He is a European rowing champion and President of the Cappoquin Rowing Club, and has just come back from a regatta in Lithuania. Anne has worked at Cappoquin House for about 25 years and, like today, I usually find her in the kitchen. She is always welcoming.

Anne leads me to the study where the fire is lit and Richard is sitting in his high-backed upright armchair reading the paper. I haven't seen Richard for more than a year. Initially he doesn't recognise me, which puts me completely at a loss. As he is rather deaf, Anne explains loudly who I am. Then he cottons on and immediately asks how Marabella is.

Despite his advanced age, to me Richard is the same as he always was—tall and distinguished with his white moustache and sharp mind. Before the Second World War Richard was a diplomatic correspondent and also the deputy editor for England's prestigious *Sunday Times* newspaper. He spent most of the war with the 10th Hussars in North Africa, under General Montgomery, fighting German Field Marshall Rommel. At one stage, Richard explains, Rommel was taken in and succeeded by a man called Von Thoma. 'I knocked down his tank and captured him,' he says gleefully.

When the war ended Richard was asked to represent the *Sunday Times* in America. He refused and came back to Cappoquin instead. 'I didn't know anything about agriculture, so I read up on it, and bought more land. It makes the size of the estate viable,' he explains.

In addition to planting the home orchard that I've just walked through, Richard established the 90-acre apple orchard, which David has taken over and developed. 'I was influenced by the fact that the Great Earl of Cork had an orchard. He was a pretty shrewd old boy,' he says with a laugh. 'I thought if he could start an orchard, why shouldn't I?'

At this point Anne comes in with some morning tea. 'I'm 99,' Richard tells me, 'and will be 100 in January. So my days are drawing to an end. All our days draw to an end sometime, but mine are drawing faster than yours.' I ask him what he is doing for his 100th birthday. 'Probably pushing up the sod!' he replies.

He makes it sound as if he is very fragile, but he obviously still has a zest for life as I notice later a small round table near the window in the dining room is laid for four. Anne tells me that he is having friends over this evening to play bridge.

Where Cappoquin House stands today is the site of Cappoquin Castle, which was built by the FitzGeralds. 'The old wall in the yard,' says Richard, 'that's the last remains of the castle.' The FitzGeralds of Dromana, Barbara Grubb's ancestors, owned Cappoquin Castle until it was taken away from them by Elizabeth I and given to Sir Christopher Hatton, a man who had danced his way to the queen's heart and went on to become Lord Chancellor of England. Sir Christopher Hatton died before the house he was building on the site of the castle was completed, but the Elizabethan east wing he constructed still stands today.

Forty years later the entrepreneurial First Earl of Cork, Richard Boyle, bought Cappoquin House and its surrounding land. He turned this area of the Blackwater valley into one of the largest centres of heavy industry in seventeenth-century Ireland. Up until then Cappoquin was just a cluster of houses around the castle. Richard Boyle found iron deposits in the area, and realised that the vast areas of woodland in West Waterford could provide the charcoal for iron smelting more cheaply than could be done in England. The Blackwater River also meant that the iron and timber could be easily transported, and water was available for the cooling process of iron production. So here at Cappoquin, where the river is still tidal, an iron works was built, which specialised in cannon manufacture.

When, in 1737, Richard's ancestor, George Keane, previously known as Seoirse O'Cathan, retired from the legal profession, he leased extensive farm and mountain lands at Cappoquin from the 4th Earl of Cork under three 999 year leases. His grandson built Cappoquin House and the Keane family have lived here for over 200 years.

Richard's father, Sir John Keane, was appointed one of the senators in the First Irish Free State in 1922. Because of his position in the new Senate, and being in favour of Ireland remaining part of Britain, Sir John was targeted by the Irish republicans who wanted full independence from Britain and Cappoquin House was set alight. The main part of the house was gutted and had to be completely rebuilt, but the Elizabethan wing survived.

Bored by talking about his father, Richard asks me about the walk and my plan to write a book about it.

The last time I attempted to write a book was at the age of nineteen when my cousin Carolyn and I decided we would write a Mills and Boon romance set in West Waterford. We worked out the plot and began with great enthusiasm. Richard took a great interest in our plans, presenting us with five Mills and Boon books. It turned out he read them on trains. Our novel never got very far, probably because we thought that our creativity was at its optimum in between one and two gin and tonics. A gin and tonic did wonders for getting us in the mood for writing. It helped us to come up with ideas and turns of phrase. But after drinking two gin and tonics we no longer felt very focused, so we didn't get much written.

Outside it starts to rain again. 'We haven't completed the harvest yet,' Richard comments. 'We've still 100 acres to do I think.' The Keanes grow wheat and oats, as well as maize to feed their dairy herd. Later in the day Juju drives me past a field of oats which hasn't been harvested, as the ground is so wet and on every attempt the tractor has sunk into the mud. 'I bought that land where we now have 200 cows,' Richard continues. 'You see, I thought the estate could only be profitable if it was made bigger, and it was a correct assumption.' He leans against the back of his chair and pauses before concluding, 'You've got to do something in life, and sometimes it comes off and sometimes it doesn't.'

His comment immediately makes me think of his orchards of apples, those symbols of choice, and the sort of life he might have had if he had gone to America with the *Sunday Times* instead of coming back to Cappoquin and expanding the estate. He had that Anglo-Irish drive, despite turbulent and economically harsh times in Ireland, to maintain his house and land.

Leaving Richard I walk down into the town of Cappoquin and I come to the two large stones on either corner of Castle Street opposite the market square. Cappoquin is known as the 'cornerstone town'. The legend is that the poet Tomás Bán FitzGerald, one of the early occupiers of Cappoquin Castle, fell on hard times because of a curse. He was paid a visit by the devil in the guise of two hellhounds. They struck a bargain with Tomás that would make him prosperous again if he would give them his firstborn son. At the time Tomás was unmarried. So, with no prospects of having children, the deal seemed to be a very good one and he agreed. The deed was written on the cornerstone of the castle's fireplace and soon his wealth was restored.

Years passed and Tomás forgot about this deal. He met and married a French noblewoman and she gave birth to their son Muiris. The hounds returned to claim the child but Tomás refused to give up his son. Not long after the boy died mysteriously and his mother died soon after of a broken heart. Devastated Tomás decided to leave Cappoquin and Ireland forever. In anger he had the cornerstone removed from the fireplace and rolled it from the castle down to where it now lies in Castle Street.

Later a similar stone was placed on the other corner. No one is quite sure which is the original one, but many emigrants from Cappoquin have chipped off a piece of the smaller of the stones on the eastern corner of Castle Street and taken it with them for good luck when they left Ireland.

Further down the street outside Kelleher's supermarket is parked a blue and white sprayed car. The names of the members of the Waterford team have been written on the roof. There are two hurleys painted on the boot and down the side of the vehicle is 'C'mon D Deise'. It has a Kilkenny numberplate, and above it is written, 'There's more than one way to skin a cat'.

As I look at the devoted decoration, I catch the eye of a man in black gumboots and a tweed cap who is standing in the doorway of Kellehers. 'Sure,' he says bitterly, 'what good is painting?'

When I get back to Tivoli House, Juju offers me a glass of her delicious apple juice made from apples from the family orchards. For the last twenty years Juju has made thousands of bottles of Crinnaghtaun Apple Juice, which are sold in delicatessens, supermarkets, hotels and restaurants across Ireland. As we sit at the kitchen table eating the remains of last night's curries, David announces that Dom Eamon Fitzgerald, the abbot of Mount Melleray Abbey, has just been elected Abbot General of the Cistercian Order. This means he will oversee the 170 Cistercian monasteries and convents around the world. David's ancestor leased the monks the land on the mountain more than 150 years ago, so there is a family connection to the monastery. Today, with the monastery's lack of younger recruits, David wonders who will take on the role of the next abbot at Mount Melleray.

33

The Road of the Saints to the Road of Slaughter

Later in the day I rejoin the Road of the Saints and after walking for five minutes reach Drumroe, the old farmhouse where I am staying tonight with the Julian and Wishy Martin. Julian has a business recycling organic waste on agricultural land and Wishy is an artist. Living, as they do, right on St Declan's Way, Julian and Wishy are both very interested in my walk, and Wishy is walking with me tomorrow. Although on my map the route is through Cappoquin, Julian explains that a little further down this road is Cooples Quay. It was here where St Declan's Way crossed the Blackwater, because in a dry summer at low tide the river is fordable.

Given the record-breaking rain of this summer, the river is definitely not fordable, but Julian asks if I would like to paddle across the river tomorrow in his canoe. Delighted at the idea of taking the original route, and as Wishy agrees to drive over with my backpack and meet us on the far bank, I instantly take up this offer. Julian is equally enthusiastic about the plan, suggesting we leave an hour and a half after low tide. It sounds simple enough. It is only when their daughter Alice points out that her father is a large man and I am quite small, and questions the stability of the canoe, that I begin to consider somewhat nervously the logistics of the operation.

When I come down to the kitchen the following morning, wearing my swimming costume and my wet weather trousers and jacket, for our 10 a.m. rendezvous, I do feel a little apprehensive. Then Julian appears and says he has already been down to the river this morning. It is flowing very fast, so he suggests that Wishy and I have a look at it. As the three of us stare at the fast-flowing mass of muddy brown water, finally Julian admits he doesn't think we should attempt the crossing after all. If we got into trouble we definitely couldn't swim against the current. I don't argue.

Before heading back to the house, I deviate along a track beside the river to look at Norrisland Castle, the home of Valentine Greatrakes, who lived here more than 350 years ago. He was famous in both England and Ireland for his healing abilities, and many people came to visit him at Norrisland. Valentine Greatrakes was known as 'the stroker' because of his method of stroking patients with his hands. On this stretch of the Road of the Saints *behauns*, little makeshift dwellings, were built along the road by people waiting to be healed. Today it's as if the fortified Jacobean house that once stood here has been consumed by nature and all that remains are a few crumbling walls and a chimney stake smothered in green ivy in the middle of a field of maize.

I'm looking forward to walking with Wishy today. Of course it would make sense for us to get going, but after Julian disappears to his office we sit back down at the kitchen table. Wishy puts the large kettle onto the Aga hob and we have another cup of coffee and talk about art. She shows me the painting she has recently done of Richard Keane. In its free, almost Impressionistic style, it catches him beautifully, sitting in his chair in the study at Cappoquin House, just as I saw him yesterday.

I only really started to get to know Wishy well last year when she held an exhibition of my father's watercolours in her studio. I'm fascinated, listening to this creative woman. She talks about the art classes she teaches and mostly she says it isn't about brush techniques, form or proportions, but rather helping people to give themselves permission to create, to stop sabotaging themselves and allow their creativity to flow.

By the time we set off at eleven the clouds are low and dark and rain looks imminent, so on the way out Wishy picks up a small black umbrella from beside the front door. The narrow road curves and bends its way towards Cappoquin and as we walk Wishy tells me about her recent visit to Plum Village in France, where the Vietnamese Buddhist monk and author Thich Nhat Hanh is based. One of the things she enjoyed most while she was there was the early morning walk she did for practising mindfulness. Then she asks if this is the pace I usually walk at. I realise it is. I have never thought about it before. Neither of us set a pace this morning, we just fell naturally into step, not going either particularly fast or slow. It's a speed at which, Wishy adds, she could walk all day.

It's wonderful to be reminded of Thich Nhat Hanh. His book *Peace is Every Step* is a favourite of mine. I love the way it offers simple ways to a more peaceful life, making the concept of peace in our busy lives do-able. Another of my treasured Thich Nhat Hanh books is *Living Buddha, Living Christ*. I first read it before Stephen and I got married, and again recently. It has given me a real understanding of the essence of Christianity as opposed to much of what we experience around the Christian message. Ireland has been severely shaken in recent years by the huge number of cases that have come to light of priests molesting children. The fact that these people are preaching one set of values and living by another is both saddening and confusing.

Wishy tells me that Andrew, her youngest son, was blessed by His Holiness The Dalai Lama when he was a baby. What really strikes home hearing her talking about her Buddhist beliefs is that every single one of us is an enormously diverse mix of ideas and beliefs. I realise I've been compartmentalising other people—thinking they are this or that sort of person. Perhaps most significantly I've been doing this to myself, boxing myself in. Over the last couple of weeks, since walking St Declan's Way, I have been trying to answer the big life question of who I am.

If I believe I should not kill, why do I eat meat? If I don't live in Ireland, how can I belong here? How can I truly love nature if I drive a car and catch planes? My mind has gone round and round in this self-critical analysis, but now

Wishy reminds me of Thich Nhat Hanh's poem, 'Call Me By My True Names', and I realise within everyone there is good and bad, pain and joy, fear and love. Suddenly, it is as if the riddle has dissolved. I am just who I am. This means I don't have to beat myself up trying to be someone that I'm not, and that my inconsistencies are a natural part of being alive. The relief of my revelation is extraordinary. I have been mulling over this ever since I started the walk, and I feel a surge of happiness just to be able to let it go. Then I realise this is one of the many gifts of walking. The gentle rhythm and the time which allows the mind to unravel some of its tangled knots. When I'm at home I often find that solutions to problems or ideas come to me when I go out for a walk for an hour, or even when I'm just walking up to the shops.

At the layby just before Cappoquin we come across Michael McCarthy, who is sitting in his car looking at the river. He's the brother of poet Thomas McCarthy, who used to regale my cousins and me with his spellbinding stories of early Lismore and ancient Ireland. I have never met Michael before. He is short in stature like his brother and I can see the family resemblance. I quickly realise he, too, is a captivating storyteller. He tells me he was a postman for sixteen years and during that time cycled 58 000 miles. The bicycle he rode belonged to the post office, so he wasn't able to keep it when he retired a few years ago. Now he has a car for leisure, but says a bicycle would be handy.

You often used to see old black bicycles propped up against the sides of cottages. It was common to see people cycling in and out of Cappoquin and Lismore as they went about their daily business. But now both towns are full of cars. The only person I have seen on a bicycle in the last few days is Mrs Aherne, an elderly lady who still cycles 2 miles into Lismore every day from the townland of Ballyanchor. 'Everyone is in such a hurry they have no time,' Michael muses, 'so they would not ride a bicycle.'

'The Celtic Tiger brought out the true nature of the Irish,' Michael continues. 'All you see is greed.' Many believe that people became very materialistic and also complacent during Ireland's great economic boom. It was thought there would be no end to this gush of gold. But now, the tide has turned, and for thousands, brought with it enormous financial hardship.

Michael stares out of his car window at the surging brown water and then tells us solemnly that the Blackwater is very dangerous at the moment because you wouldn't know what might be floating in it. I'm just pleased that Julian and I didn't attempt the canoe crossing. We could well have been overturned and be bobbing downstream at this very moment.

It starts to rain so I dive into my waterproof trousers and jacket, and Wishy puts up her small black umbrella.

On the far side of Cappoquin Wishy points out a stone plaque on the pavement which says:

Robert (Linen) Cooke
c1646–c1726
Man of Property
Vegan and Eccentric

We're now on Cooke Street, which is named after the said Robert Cooke who did not eat fish, flesh, milk or butter, or drink alcohol. He didn't wear woollen clothes or any other animal produce, which was a very radical step at that time. This clothier and landowner was known by locals as Linen Cooke, because he only wore white linen. It makes me think about how we often take the exploitation of animals for granted, especially as many of us get our meat neatly packaged off supermarket shelves. Linen Cooke reminds me that it is quite possible to live to a ripe old age without killing animals.

Further along Cooke Street I wonder if Linen is turning in his grave because of the battery farming at Cappoquin Chickens. A few vans are parked on the premises, and one or two people are walking around, but otherwise the place looks empty. Apparently, a British-based poultry company visited last week, but doesn't have enough money to buy the business. In an effort to save the hundreds of jobs it provides, local farmers are trying to buy the company.

The rain gets heavier and heavier as we leave the outskirts of town and pass the spot where Julian and I were to have landed in the canoe. This is not the soft misty Irish rain that I love, but a downpour. Already, the rain has permeated my boots and my socks are soggy. It looks like the expected deluge after Hurricane Hanna has arrived, just as Nick Trigg predicted.

St Declan's Way turns to the left here, but first we walk a short distance along the road straight ahead to the Finisk River and my favourite bridge in the world. Hanging in the hall at home I have an exquisite watercolour of it that my father did for me. What I particularly love about this bridge is its gatehouse folly at the far end, which is not only beautiful, but totally unexpected. The middle of rural Ireland is the last place you'd expect to come across a Hindu Gothic-style gate lodge with a big copper blue dome and minarets, and slender arched pointed windows. Every time I go through its narrow archway I feel as if I am passing into another world.

This spectacular edifice marks the old entrance to the Dromana estate and was originally built nearly 200 years ago in papier-mâché by the people who lived and worked on the Dromana estate to celebrate the marriage of my friend Barbara Grubb's ancestor, Henry Villiers-Stuart to Austrian beauty Theresa Pauline Ott. It was inspired by John Nash's famous pavilion in Brighton where the couple had spent their honeymoon. They liked the gate lodge so much, they later had it built in stone to give local people work during the famine in 1849.

Perhaps what makes the gatehouse so incongruous is that the great wedding it was constructed to honour turned out to be a sham. Unknown to Henry his new wife—referred to by Barbara as 'Hot Ott'—already had a husband and two children in Austria. Not only was poor Henry blackmailed to keep the shame of this under wraps, the legitimacy of his own subsequent children was called into question and his newly won hereditary title of Baron Stuart de Decies was never passed on to his son.

As we stand in the pouring rain looking at the bridge, Julian calls Wishy on her mobile to see if she wants to be picked up. While she is talking I walk across the bridge and discover one of the doors in the archway of the gate lodge has a broken lock. I push it open and find myself in the little room with its red brick walls. It is completely dry in here, and such a relief for a moment to be out of the rain. There is an identical room on the other side of the archway: one was the gatekeeper's day room and the other the night room.

Barbara told me that when King Edward VII was staying with the Duke and Duchess of Devonshire at Lismore Castle in 1904, he decided to visit Dromana. Wanting to be low-key he came in a jaunting car. When the king arrived at the gate lodge, the gatekeeper asked him for his pass, as everyone entering Dromana had to have a pass. The king said he didn't have one, so the gatekeeper told him to be gone. Horrified when they later discovered the king had been turned away, the Villiers-Stuart family questioned the gatekeeper. He stressed that he'd been told not to let anyone in without a pass. Then he added, 'You told me if I ever saw a suspicious-looking fella not to let him in, and I never saw a more suspicious-looking fella in my life.'

Wishy tells Julian she'll keep going so we push on through the driving rain. A couple of miles beyond the bridge is Dromana, the tower house perched on the cliff above the Blackwater that was recently left to Barbara by her father, James Villiers-Stuart. But we're not going to Dromana today and instead turn left onto *Boheravagheragh*, the Road of Slaughter.

34

Deluge

Boheravagheragh got its name because it was along here that the Battle of Affane took place between the FitzGeralds and another Old English family, the Butlers. Gerald FitzGerald, the Earl of Desmond, and Thomas Butler, the Earl of Ormond, were each heads of Old English families and both wanted to increase their power bases. Thomas Butler was actually Gerald Fitzgerald's stepson, but they hated each other and had previously nearly gone to war over some land in Tipperary. They met on the road here with their respective private armies. A battle ensued and 300 men were killed before the Earl of Desmond was thrown off his horse and shot in the thigh. Wounded and collapsed on the ground Gerald FitzGerald was carried off on the back of one of the Butlers. Soon Ormond's army started goading FitzGerald and shouting, 'Where is the great Earl of Desmond now?' To which he quickly replied, 'Where, but in his rightful place, on the necks of the Butlers.'

Queen Elizabeth I summoned both the earls to London. Initially, the queen was even-handed in her administration of justice. But at the end of the day blood is thicker than water and Ormond was after all the queen's cousin and a favourite of hers. Later she blamed the Earl of Desmond and his brother, John, for the Battle of Affane and had them arrested.

With their leader locked up, other members of the FitzGerald clan decided to take matters into their own hands. They rebelled against the English and Ormond, and after the Earl of Desmond and his brother were released, they rebelled again. Initially, Gerald FitzGerald did not want to collaborate with the rebels, but once he was proclaimed a traitor by the English authorities he joined the rebel forces. He was eventually hunted down and killed in the mountains of Kerry by the local clan O'Moriarty, who received 1000 pounds of silver for the Earl of Desmond's head, which was sent to the queen herself.

Queen Elizabeth then decided that the lands of the Earl of Desmond and his allies should be given to English settlers to ensure that similar rebellions against the crown did not occur again. Known as the Munster plantations, thousands of English soldiers and administrators who had played a part in quelling the rebellion, including Sir Walter Raleigh, were allocated land.

As we walk along this quiet country road, with fields on one side and woodlands on the other, it is hard to imagine that Affane was once a key administrative and business centre in County Waterford. In medieval times large fairs were held here three times a year which attracted people from miles around. Poignantly, now all that remains is the ruined Affane Church and its graveyard.

Julian rings Wishy again to say that he is going to Foley's Bar in Lismore for lunch. As it is now raining so heavily he asks if she wants to come. Stoically, she suggests we walk on a bit further along the road to River Valley Plants, the nursery run by Maurice Hogan, where we can at least eat our lunch out of the rain.

We pass a field of bulrushes and Wishy points out an alder. Growing near water the alder is believed to be the tree of the water spirits. Its wood, which becomes stronger and harder when immersed in water, was traditionally used to make shields. When the wood is cut, it turns from white to red, which is why it was thought to be a tree of war and death. In Ireland alders are considered unlucky. It is especially unlucky to pass an alder on a journey.

Plodding through the bucketing rain with increasingly dampened spirits, I just hope the negative effect of the alder can be counteracted by the traveller's joy, with its creamy spider-like flowers, climbing along the dry stone wall beside the road.

When Julian rings for the third time we still haven't reached River Valley Plants and Wishy finally concedes defeat. With her jeans wet through and her little black umbrella doing a pathetic job of keeping her dry, I can't blame her. Fifteen minutes later Julian pulls up in his four-wheel drive. I am determined to get some miles behind me today, so I'm not tempted to jump in with them. But within moments I am missing Wishy. When she was walking beside me, it felt like a bit of a lark being out on this dreadful day, now I feel momentarily bereft, left alone in the rain.

It's about a mile and a half along this quiet stretch of road known as *Casan na Naomh*, the Path of the Saints, before I see a sign for the nursery. I walk up the drive and find a brown papier-mâché horse looking out from a small glasshouse attached to a house. There's no one home but a man working out the back tells me the nursery is next door. I pass a couple of large greenhouses with brambles and nettles growing out of their broken windows, then reach a very long high-roofed glasshouse. Down the far end two men are potting plants. One turns out to be the owner, Maurice. In true Irish spirit he looks totally unfazed when I introduce myself and explain that Wishy suggested I came here for lunch. However, I realise lunch guests are not usually the order of the day, as Maurice immediately goes off in search of a chair and returns with an upright wooden one with a large hole in it. The seat cover has ripped and the foam padding worn away. So he then hunts around for a rag to put in the gap, sits me down, and promptly disappears.

I take off my jacket and discover, despite my wide-brimmed hat, the driving rain has gone down my neck, and my 100 per cent waterproof trousers are not quite as impermeable as they promised. Wet and despondent I slowly eat my sandwich, listening to the sound of water dripping through the roof and watching puddles form on the concrete floor. The wind and rain lashes against the glass, and I dread the thought of having to go back out into it. In the far corner of the huge glasshouse, the other man silently continues potting.

Eventually I drag myself back into the weather, and this time I put the hood of my jacket up under my broad-brimmed hat. No doubt I look utterly ridiculous, but at this stage I'm past caring, and at least I'm drier.

Very soon I arrive at the small village of Kilmolash, with its ruined abbey and surrounding graveyard. In the First Earl of Cork's time, this was a major parish. The abbey is strategically positioned by River Finisk and more than 1000 years ago was raided by the Vikings. Like Affane it is now another bit of forgotten Ireland.

The intensity of the rain increases and large puddles of water are spreading across the road, just as I pass a business selling solar water heating systems. A large sign promises to provide 70 per cent of a home's hot water and 100 per cent in summer. I can't help but wonder whether this year people have been forced to give up washing or are having a lot of cold baths.

When it seems like the rain will never end, it eases. St Declan's Way turns up a boreen with purple prickly headed teasels growing on its banks. Much to my surprise, at the top of this narrow grassy track, next to a farm gate, is a brown metal sign saying, 'St Declan's Way'. It's just like the signs I saw between Cashel and Cahir. I dwell for a moment on its auspiciousness.

But my optimism dissolves when I see that the sign points to the left, while on my map it looks as if the path curls to the right and up to a woodland. There's a cluster of trees straight ahead, so assuming that is the woodland, I follow an electric fence up the side of the field. But halfway up the field the electric wire crosses in front of the path. I must have made a mistake so I return to the gate.

The sign points to an impassable path on the left. So on my second attempt I walk to the right, along the bottom of the field and through the next field, until I meet a farm track. I'm following this up the hill, uncertain of whether I'm going the right way, when I see a track below me on the left. I'm sure it's St Declan's Way. I try to get down to it, but the brambles are so thick it is impossible. I have no alternative but to walk further up the hill until I find a gap through the undergrowth. I climb over a barbed wire fence and scramble down onto what is essentially a narrow path with high banks on either side.

I'm so busy negotiating the barbed wire and brambles, it isn't until my feet hit the ground that I look up to find myself face to face with a herd of bullocks. Bullocks are curious creatures and love a bit of excitement, such as a person on a walk. This path is only wide enough for one bullock. I quickly realise the ones at the back will probably jostle the ones in front to get a better look. It's not a happy prospect. The likely outcome would be bullocks shunting forward and me being flattened.

This isn't the time to sit and ponder, I need to make a decision and quickly. I contemplate running as fast as I can up the track, but then remember bullocks love a good chase. I look at the bank and wonder if I can climb back up, but it is much too high and steep. With rising panic, as the young Friesians stare inquisitively at me and take a couple of steps closer, I have no idea what to do. So in the sternest voice I can muster, I turn to face the frisky bullocks and say, very firmly, 'Go back!' I think St Declan must be looking after me, because much to my surprise and great relief they obediently turn tail and head back down the hill. Perhaps I shouldn't be so amazed. St Declan is known to have performed quite a few miracles.

One day on his journey back to Ireland from Rome Declan was saying mass in a church when a little black bell floated through the window of the church and landed on the altar before him. Thinking this bell came from heaven, he gave thanks for it, and took it with him. After that many miracles occurred because of this little bell. When Declan arrived at the English Channel, he did not have enough money for a ship to make the crossing. So he struck the bell and prayed to God for help. Shortly afterwards an empty sail-less ship appeared. Declan and his followers went aboard and it floated to harbour in England, where they disembarked and watched it float away again.

Relieved to have survived the bullock encounter I continue on the muddy path, which has been well-trodden by the cattle, until it comes to a laneway. St Declan's Way goes straight across, but marked on the map not far up this lane is the site of three ancient cooking places. Curious to look at them I follow the lane up the hill until I find myself in a farmyard. I walk round to the back door of the house, hoping to find someone to ask about the cooking places. There is a sign on the window saying, 'Beware of the Dog. Enter at your own risk.' I knock, but there's neither dog or owner, and no obvious ancient cooking places either.

However, as I'm leaving, a girl drives up in a car. This is her family's farm, she says, but she knows nothing about the ancient cooking places. Then she warns me that where St Declan's Way crosses the stream below is very wet and muddy. Given my feet have not been dry since leaving Drumroe this morning, I'm not overly concerned. But after wading through the stream, because it is too swollen to jump over, I realise my feet were actually much drier than I thought. Now they are absolutely sodden.

The wind is still roaring, but thankfully it's hardly raining now. Looking at the map I see St Declan's Way rejoins a minor road, which I follow until I come to a turning to Aglish. There is a bed and breakfast marked on the map here and it's where I plan to stay the night. As I approach Aglish I hear the angelus bell ringing from the Catholic church and realise it is six o'clock. As well as being a call to prayer, the angelus bell apparently spreads goodwill to everyone on earth. Hearing it as I walk into the village, after a day of battling the elements, is a wonderful welcome.

One thing I learnt long ago is that if you don't know where you're going in Ireland, ask a publican or a priest. So I head into the Elephant Bar, and ask the barman for directions to the bed and breakfast. He looks a little perplexed, which is slightly alarming as there can't be more than one or two B&Bs here. He suggests enquiring at the petrol station. So I walk back down the hill. The two women working there tell me there is no bed and breakfast in Aglish. Unsure of what to do next I ask the women where the closest B&B is. 'Cappoquin or Clashmore,' one replies abruptly.

I don't know whether to laugh or cry. Here I am, completely soaked and exhausted, and I've just been told the nearest bed and breakfast is about 8 miles away. I am standing in the petrol station praying for help, but neither of these women appears moved by my predicament. Then a man with a rolling right eye walks in. He tells me there is a B&B near Dromana and he is driving to Villierstown so can give me a lift. I ring the B&B from the petrol station's pay phone. The woman who answers tells me she has a spare room but does not do dinner, so I buy a tin of baked beans. Once again I feel blessed.

Being tired as well as wet, I feel so grateful to this man, John Poyner, for giving me a lift. But as we speed northwards back towards Dromana, I am horribly aware that most of the ground I covered today is being lost. John asks if I would like him to drive me to Cappoquin, but I can't bear the thought of having got no further along St Declan's Way at all, or the embarrassment of turning up again on Juju and David's doorstep looking even more bedraggled than before.

I ask him to drop me at the top of the Dromana drive, just in case Barbara has come over from Castle Grace, or her mother Emily is there. I ring the doorbell but no one is home, so I walk down the road to the modern bungalow with the green shamrock sign outside indicating that it's a B&B approved by the Bord Failte tourism authority. It's then I remember the alder. I now believe that alders are unlucky. I've walked all day in the wind and the rain and I am now almost back where I started, a few miles south of Cappoquin.

35

Turkeys and chickens

The first question John and Mary Nugent who run the bed and breakfast ask is where am I from? When I explain, Mary tells me my mother bought a turkey from her one Christmas. I am a little confused because I know we used to get our turkeys from Sarah Tobin in Tallow. I say as much, and Mary replies that Sarah, who died of cancer several years ago, was her sister.

Sarah Tobin was a small energetic woman with great spirit. Though I haven't thought about her in ages, I liked Sarah from the first moment I met her, which was when I went one year with my father to collect the turkey. But my opinion quickly changed when she took one look at me and said to my father, 'She's not half as fine a woman as her mother.'

Admittedly, Marabella is a good-looking woman, but I thought Sarah's words were really not in the spirit of Christmas. I said nothing at the time, but I could not get her harsh remark out of my head. When we were eating the turkey on Christmas Day, I mentioned rather crossly what she had said. My mother roared with laughter and explained that by 'fine' she meant 'big'. Suddenly I liked Sarah a whole lot more.

As she puts all my wet clothes to dry in front of the Aga, Mary says that Sarah and she were from a family of thirteen children: two boys and eleven girls. Then, despite the no dinner policy, she asks me to sit down at the kitchen table and kindly makes me a ham sandwich and some tea, and heats up the tin of baked beans I bought in Aglish. She tells me that she saw me walking out of Cappoquin with Wishy this morning. John and she have at least one person a year staying who is walking St Declan's Way. Having walked more than three-quarters of the route without meeting another pilgrim, it is comforting to hear that at least someone wanders the Way occasionally.

When I've eaten John and Mary invite me to sit with them in front of the turf fire. The Nugents have 50 acres of land on which they keep a dairy herd of 40 cows. I ask if I can see the cows being milked in the morning. They also have two chicken houses. The houses are empty at the moment, because the chickens all went off last week. Due to the financial crisis at Cappoquin Chickens, the Nugents aren't actually sure if they will be paid. But Mary quickly adds, 'Luckily, our six children are all reared and we have no loans.'

John is originally a mountainy man and grew up on the Knockmealdowns near Castle Doddard. He used to go to the castle as a child to pick hurts. He left the mountain 45 years ago, when he swapped 120 acres up there for these 50 acres of better land. His family's house on the mountain did not have electricity. They cooked on an open fire, and took a bucket to the well to get water. They had cattle and grew potatoes and turnips. Back then, he says, one family would kill a pig and the other neighbouring families would eat it with them. I like John. He has a twinkly face and radiant smile, and tells me that when he was a child living on the mountain he used to wear no shoes in summer.

John's family were originally on Ussher land, he tells me, but were evicted and moved up the mountain during the famine. It was the Kiely-Usshers who built the Towers at Ballysaggartmore, and were renowned for the bad treatment of their tenants during the famine.

I read an article written by a reporter from the *Cork Examiner*, who was sent to the Lismore area to report on the effects of the famine. The reporter describes the dreadful hardships that people like John's family would have suffered:

> Arriving at Ballysaggartmore an awful sight was before my eyes, I found twelve to fourteen houses levelled to the ground. The walls of a few were still standing but the roofs were taken off, the windows broken in, and the doors removed. Groups of famished women and crying children still hovered round the place of their birth, endeavouring to find shelter from the piercing cold of the mountain blast, cowering near the ruins or seeking refuge beneath the chimneys. The cow, the house, the wearing apparel, the furniture, and even in extreme cases the bed clothes were pawned to support existence. As I have been informed the

whole tenantry, amounting with their families to over 700 persons, on the Ballysaggartmore estate, are proscribed.

John, Mary and I talk for a while before I go to my room. There is a holy water holder on the wall just next to the door. Above the bed is a picture of the Sacred Heart of Mary in a large gold frame. In the middle of her bosom is a red heart with a sword through it and a string of white roses around it. Out of the top of the heart is what looks like a puff of white smoke, which I know symbolises Mother Mary's deep love of God and mankind. It's touching to see this symbol of faith but as a non-Catholic I have to admit it's hard for me to make the connection.

As I get into bed I think of my day and particularly the time spent walking with Wishy. Little do I know that in eight months she will discover she has an inoperable brain tumour, and after a painful struggle, she will die just over a year later. I feel so grateful for the gift of inspiration she blessed me with today. How precious are the moments we spend in true connection with another person, and as Wishy was so aware, how important it is to be completely present when spending time with our friends and loved ones.

36

Dromana

By the time I am up and dressed the next morning the milking is nearly over. I walk down to the dairy to find John and his son, Martin, moving quietly between the last of the cows standing in the stalls. The radio is on, which, John says, helps calm the animals. I watch the milk being pumped from their udders into a large glass bottle. The cows yield between 6 and 7 gallons, depending on the weather, and the milk is picked up every three days and taken to the creamery in Kilkenny.

On my way back to the house I pass the two chicken houses. Mary tells me they were built about twenty years ago and 19 000 chickens are reared in each house. Rearing chickens must have given the Nugents essential income for bringing up their six children, but when I look at the houses and imagine 19 000 birds in each one I can't help wondering what sort of existence those battery-reared chickens would have had in that confined and artificial environment.

Mary tells me that John and she have a meeting with Cappoquin Chickens tomorrow, when they will hear what the future is for the company and also where they stand in terms of payment. John, Mary and Martin have breakfast at the kitchen table, but being a paying guest I am directed to the front room, where a place is set for me at the head of the dining table. I sit with my back to the window, looking at the china figurines, the cabinet of cut glass and bone china, and the photographs of the family. For my tea is a jug of fresh milk straight from the dairy.

My plan today was to walk from Aglish to Ardmore, which, including the detour to St Declan's Well of Toor near Geosh, is about 14 miles. However, I'm now more than 7 miles from Aglish. I should just get walking, but of course I don't. Instead, I turn down the Dromana drive, past the sign advertising the times the house and gardens are open to the public, to see if anyone is in. This time I find Barbara and Georgina, her daughter, in the final stages of preparing for the 22 people from An Taisce, the National Trust for Ireland, who are coming to stay for three days.

Dromana is perched on a cliff high up above the Blackwater. The stone tower house was built in the 1200s and the castle and its land came into the FitzGeralds' possession in the first half of the thirteenth century. Barbara is a direct descendant of the Earl of Desmond's son, who first moved here in the 1400s. But the name FitzGerald lost its association with Dromana more than 300 years ago, when Katherine, the only daughter of John FitzGerald, became heir to the family lands and titles. Seeing an opportunity to obtain the Dromana estate, her relative Lord Power, pressed the thirteen-year-old Katherine into a marriage with his son, who was then only seven years old. A couple of years later, realising the motives for this union, Katherine repudiated the marriage and, despite it not yet having been annulled, she married Edward Villiers.

Five times in the last 300 years Dromana and its land have been passed through the female line. Most recently was after James Villiers-Stuart's death in 2004, when it was left to Barbara.

It was here at Dromana that the Countess of Desmond, who, it is said, lived to be 140 years old, died after falling out of a tree. This lady, who in her youth is believed to have danced at court with the future Richard III, married the Twelfth Earl of Desmond at the beginning of the sixteenth century and when he died 30 years later she moved to Inchiquin Castle near Youghal. After the Desmond Rebellions the castle and its lands were granted to Sir Walter Raleigh. He allowed the countess to stay at Inchiquin, but when later it became the property of Richard Boyle, he persistently tried to evict her.

It is also said that at the age of about 130, the countess set off from Youghal with her daughter, who was more than 90, and travelled on foot, pushing her daughter in a cart, from Bristol to London, where she went to James I's court and put forward her case to keep her lands and succeeded. Apparently, not long before her death she grew a new set of teeth. One report says her death came after falling out of a nut tree, but locally it is believed that she died at Dromana after falling out of a cherry tree given to her by Sir Walter Raleigh.

In the hall are large Georgian portraits of Villiers-Stuart ancestors with their characteristic long noses and the same rounded jaw as Barbara. A row of fox heads are mounted on the wall of the passage to the loo, and in the hallway five swords are sitting in the umbrella stand beside the walking sticks and a couple of riding crops. On one walking stick is a silver band with an engraving that says the stick was cut from the cherry tree planted by Sir Walter Raleigh in 1582.

There is also a particularly fine sword with a silver scabbard. On the blade is a crown and underneath are the initials IVS, which stand for Ion Villiers-Stuart. This was Barbara's grandfather. Despite being refused entry to the gates of Dromana, King Edward VII apparently gave the sword to Ion at the time of his visit to Ireland.

Dromana has its fair share of colourful tales. Edward Villiers, who three centuries ago married Katherine FitzGerald, haunts the house. Emily, Barbara's mother, saw him surrounded by a mist on the landing one night when she was pregnant. She was absolutely terrified, let out a piercing scream and leapt down about eight stairs and into her husband's arms.

There is a painting of Edward Villiers and his Moorish page on the wall in the drawing room, and it is said that Edward bled the boy to death to see if it was a painful way of leaving this world. But that is not the only lurid story about Edward Villiers. Apparently, an old widow, who was one of the Dromana tenants, had two sons who were always quarrelling. In desperation she took her sons to Edward and begged him to try and make peace between them. He promptly hanged one son and sent the other one back to his mother with a message to say there would be no more quarrels. The widow then put a curse on Edward and his descendants for the next four generations.

Barbara also told me that one night there was a dinner party at Dromana, and during the course of the evening James, Barbara's father, went outside with his father Ion and stepbrother Peter Patrick. As they stood in the dark James heard the sound of the banshee, but Peter Patrick, not being a blood relation, did not. Banshees are solitary female fairies whose wailing and keening forewarn of an imminent death in old Irish families. Each banshee has her own mortal family for which she has a fierce and passionate caring. Later that night Ion Villiers-Stuart had a heart attack and died aged only 49.

James was still a minor when his father died. When he did take over Dromana a couple of years later, there was very little money and the farmable land was only about 600 acres. Less than 100 years earlier Dromana had been an estate of about 30 000 acres.

The Dromana estate included all the houses in Villierstown, which had been built when the family set up the linen industry there in the 1700s, but they were yielding low rents due to the rent restrictions act, and also facing home improvement orders. James could not afford to keep those houses as they were a financial liability. So he went down the village with the deed of transfer for the house in one hand and a 5-pound note in the other. First, he gave the 5-pound note as a present to each tenant, and then asked if they would like to take the property on and all its liability. When they signed the deed, he took back the 5 pounds as payment.

Eventually, in 1957, James had to sell Dromana. Barbara and her sister, Caroline, were born here and when Dromana was sold the family never thought they would return. But nearly 40 years later James and Emily were able to buy it back, and once again live in the place which has been the family home for more than 700 years.

Barbara and Georgina are about to head off to the market in Dungarvan, so Barbara makes coffee and we sit for a few minutes at the round table by the window in the kitchen. I look down at the Blackwater rolling past below us. Its shiny grey mud flats are now exposed because the tide is low. For a moment a kestrel hovers next to the window before it turns and disappears out of sight. As Barbara starts to move around the kitchen again and Georgina begins to add additional items to the long list she is holding, I leave them to it, and, at Barbara's suggestion, walk through the garden down to the river.

At the far end of the lawn I turn back and look at the Jacobean house and try to imagine what it must have looked like 50 years ago, before the Georgian section which included a large ballroom, was pulled down.

I follow the Lady's Walk through the woodlands until I reach the oak tree. According to tradition, I walk clockwise around it and make a wish. Below here is the Banqueting House. Fallen leaves carpet the floor of this little stone building where the ladies used to picnic while their men were fishing. In the main room, with its big fireplace, the remains of a rusty wheelbarrow sit upside-down beside a moss-covered tree trunk lying diagonally across the room. But most extraordinary is the graffiti, some of which is centuries old on the walls of the two smaller rooms.

Walking along the river bank back towards the house I reach the bastion, which originally was an outer fortification and now houses a long wooden canoe, and the oars for the large heavy rowing boat, known as the 'Old Cow', that is currently resting on the mud flats.

The sky was blue earlier this morning, but now as I head into Villierstown it starts to rain again. This village, with its wide main streets, was built by John Villiers more than 250 years ago to develop a linen industry. It was populated with linen weavers from Lurgan in County Armagh in the north of Ireland, a place renowned for its linen manufacturing.

The door of the church is open, so I go in. At the far end is a beautiful stained-glass window, but there are no pews, nor is there an altar. I wonder what has happened to the Church of Ireland this time. There are a couple of people in the church and a man called James Roynane explains that there are still occasionally services here, but that it is now also used as a community hall.

James Roynane is part of a Fas scheme, the government initiative to get people back into the workforce, which does landscaping and gardening locally. Because it's raining the group isn't working this morning. At the back of the church is a kitchen area, where a couple of women are boiling a kettle and putting out mugs. Another woman arrives with a carton of milk and packets of Jammy Dodgers, and someone else appears with an apple pie she has just bought from the store in the nearby village of Clashmore.

When they hear I am walking St Declan's Way, they press me to have morning tea with them and a woman called Tracy offers to drive me to Aglish. So rather than tramping on in the rain I join them. It turns out the apple pie is mouldy, so we stand about drinking large mugs of tea and eating the biscuits.

There is a heated discussion about where the council has put their signs, as one has been placed in a flower bed, which the group doesn't approve of at all. Then conversation turns to the weather and someone tells us that her 96-year-old friend in Aglish, who still plays cards and doesn't need glasses, has never in her long life experienced a summer as wet as this.

Finally, talk comes round to the hurling and one woman describes her husband apoplectic with anger when watching the Déise playing on Sunday. 'They've had 50 years to prepare and look at them,' he exclaimed in disgust. 'And it'll be another 50 years before they play again!'

37

The Bog of Hags and the holy well

Tracy drops me at the top of Aglish village and by the time I have bought a sandwich from the petrol station and actually set off, it is half past twelve, which makes me worry that I haven't left myself enough time to reach Ardmore before dark. According to the map, rather than retracing my steps, I can head through Aglish and rejoin St Declan's Way by turning off the main road and up a boreen. However, an hour later I'm backtracking along the main road having been unable to find the turning, to the ironic sound of a cockerel crowing.

Eventually, at 1.40 p.m. I'm back on St Declan's Way, which almost immediately leaves the tarred road and follows a boreen then narrows to a path overgrown with nettles, brambles and ivy. The rain is off and on, and now I'm even more worried about time.

Sharp, straight rays of sunlight shine through the grey cloud. At one point the slurry is so deep on a track going up to a farm, I walk through the field beside it. By a high dry stone wall are two wooden posts with the figure of a man with a walking stick and an arrow painted on each to indicate the way. Further along, when the Way joins the main road at Geosh, there are another two signs, brown metal ones on a steel post, each pointing in opposite directions indicating the way to Cashel and Ardmore. After so few signposts until now, it appears that the rest of my journey to Ardmore will be clearly marked.

It is raining again when I cross the stone bridge over the Geosh River, and I see the handwritten sign saying 'Holy Well', and an arrow pointing up a side road to the left. This is St Declan's Well of Toor, which Michael McGrath told me about. Initially St Declan's Way follows the same road as the one up to the well, but then turns off onto a boreen. According to the map if I continue along this boreen I can take what looks like a farm track from it up to the well, and save myself over a mile.

Walking through long wet grass, I pass clumps of spearmint and a rusty cattle trough. In a field ahead is a flock of about 50 seagulls, which all fly off into the now blue sky as I approach. A herd of bullocks gallops up to the fence beside me, then they moo at me when I stop to drink some water.

The boreen takes me through the townland of Monagally, which in Irish is *Móin na gCailleach*, the Bog of the Hags. Here, hawthorn trees are covered in red berries. Also known as the fairy thorn, because fairies live in them, hawthorns have always been regarded with both fear and respect. Seeing one can mean bad luck and also a missed opportunity. Finches dive in and out of the ivy encircling one of these trees and a single magpie flies across the hillside. One for sorrow, I think, saluting the bird with a wave of my hand, as my father always did to counteract its negative impact. Not that it works—At just that moment the waist strap on my backpack breaks at the seam. So the backpack, which up to now has been snugly fitted to my back, is hanging off my shoulders and as a result much heavier. I walk on a bit but it is now so cumbersome and uncomfortable that I have to stop and put together a makeshift tie with a piece of string.

I have been walking steadily uphill and am now on mountain land among bell heather and yellow-flowering gorse. I walk and walk, but there is no sign of the track that will take me up to the well. Finally, I reach an electric fence, get a shock as I duck under it, and find myself on a narrow mountain road.

Flummoxed as to why I have reached this road instead of the track, I'm just about to knock on the door of a cottage to find out where I am when a car drives up. When I ask for directions the couple inside tell me that if I want to go to Toor Well, I'll need to follow the road down the hill, go back to Geosh and then up the mountain from there. Meanwhile I'm jabbing my map, which by this stage I have stuck through the window of their car, and insisting that the well must be somewhere very near to here. Again they tell me the circuitous road route is the only way there. The thought of having to walk another four and a half miles makes me nearly apoplectic with frustration. I continue stabbing at the map and insisting that I must be nearly there, while they hold that I'm not. Eventually, probably thinking it is the only possible way to get rid of this ranting woman and to continue on their pleasant afternoon drive, the man asks if would I like a lift to the well.

'Yes,' I say immediately, and within seconds have plonked myself in the back of their car. The retired Scottish couple in the car have recently moved to the area, they say. I assume that's why they've never heard of the track I've been looking for through the fields. Ten minutes later they leave me up the mountain at the well. Very grateful for the lift I watch the car drive away. Then, despite having walked for days across the Irish countryside on my own, I suddenly feel strangely unsettled being left alone here.

Still trying to work out why I couldn't find the track and if I have just been foxed by fairies or jinxed by bog hags, I walk through a gate beside a golden yew. Having battled through the brambles and nettles at St Declan's birthplace, I'm astonished to see in front of me a large beautifully kept area with grass lawns and gravel paths. In the middle on a high podium is a large white statue of St Declan in his bishop's garb holding his crozier, and next to this is a green and white painted pulpit beside a little white chapel with a small cross on the top of the roof and a green arched wooden door. Further down the hill is a white statue of the Virgin Mary, beside which pots of plants have been placed. And below that two wells, one for drinking from and the other underneath a chapel for washing in.

Kieran Heffernan told me he remembers walking up through the fields to the well as a child. The well came about, so the story goes, because St Declan was walking up the mountain one day, and he passed a woman with a basket of eggs. He was hungry and asked the woman if he could have one of the eggs. She said 'No', and from that day her hens never laid again.

Further up the mountain he passed a woman with a bucket of milk. As he was thirsty he asked if he could have a little milk. The woman said 'No', she needed all the milk for her children. That night her cows dried up and never produced a drop of milk again.

Then St Declan passed a woman carrying water, and asked if he could have some water, to which the woman replied, 'Certainly'. He drank the water and the woman explained that she had to go all the way down the mountain every day to collect it. St Declan told her she would never have to go down the mountain for water again. Then he struck the ground with his staff and immediately a spring appeared.

Not only did the spring appear, Kieran said, but it also produced holy water, so many people came to it and were cured of their diseases.

Later, I discover that this place is so well looked after because 60 years ago a man from Dungarvan called Jerry Fitzgerald, who was a bicycle repairer, got a spoke in his eye, and not only did it affect that eye, but also the other one, and he started to lose his sight. Jerry thought there was no hope, then someone said to him it was a pity that St Declan's Well was no longer there. Desperate for a cure he went up the mountain and managed to find the well in the undergrowth, and when he bathed his eyes with the water his sight improved dramatically. He was so thankful he spent a great deal of time and money improving the surroundings of the well and also obtained the support of Waterford County Council for its upkeep.

For more than half a century hundreds of people have come to this spot for a mass held here every July during St Declan's pattern week. Pattern comes from the Irish word pátrún meaning 'patron', as in patron saint, and refers to the saint's feast day. Typically, a pattern involves ceremonies and devotional practices at a holy well of the saint.

On the podium below the statue of St Declan is a sign quoting Reverend P Power, the man who did so much research into St Declan and St Declan's Way nearly 100 years ago:

> No Irish saint perhaps has so strong a local hold as Declan or has left so abiding a popular memory. Nevertheless his period is one of the great disputed questions of early Irish history. In traditional popular regard Declan in the Decies has ever stood first, foremost, and pioneer. Declan, whencesoever or whenever he came, is regarded as the spiritual father to whom the Déisi owe the gift of faith.

I stare at those words and realise that, in fact, very little is known for sure about St Declan.

All along my journey I have been gathering facts and information, hoping, I suppose, to be able to put all the pieces of the puzzle together to reveal the truth. But seeing this is like having a rug pulled from under me. Reading these words it hits me that this saint, whose life and history I thought I knew, might actually be someone quite different. Suddenly, I am faced with the realisation that I am never going to know the truth about St Declan.

Faced with the reality that it is an impossible quest, I feel as if I have been stripped of the sense and purpose of this walk.

I sit on the raised concrete slab next to the Virgin Mary and weep with tiredness and frustration. The frustration of not having the answers and knowing the outcomes. I wanted a neat happy ending. I wanted to reach the end of St Declan's Way with all the answers about St Declan, but more importantly I wanted to be clear about my own faith and beliefs. I wanted to be absolute in my knowing.

But instead, here I am, with the white statues of Mary and Declan looking down on me, feeling I know nothing at all, and that I have just been robbed of all the thoughts and ideas that previously gave me a modicum of certainty.

Then, as the tears roll down my face, a small black cat appears and sits in the grass among the dandelions and the thrift, gazing intently at me with its large green eyes. In Irish folklore it is said that cats had the faculties of speech and human reason, and the power of foretelling future events. They were also said to guard hidden treasures. There are no houses near here, so who knows where this one has come from. Its sudden appearance is very mysterious. But the presence of this furry black creature is like a reminder of the magical workings of life which can never be truly explained or comprehended.

I eat my sandwich then fill a black and white china mug, which has been left beside the well, with some water and drink it. Before I leave I tie a red and white spotted handkerchief to an ash tree, beside the socks, ribbons and rags already hanging there, to be worn away in the wind and the rain with my concerns and worries.

38

Stepping stones

Kieran Heffernan described to me walking up to the well on a narrow path between the hedgerows and I notice a kissing gate leading out onto what looks like a path that will take me back down the mountain to St Declan's Way. Initially, it seems promising, but after about 50 yards the path peters out in a field of nettles, and terrified of getting lost in the vortex of the Bog of Hags, I decide to turn around and take the long way back via the road.

Half an hour later I'm back on St Declan's Way, and once again I walk through the long grass, past the rusty trough, and again the herd of bullocks congregates to look at me. But this time, instead of heading east up the mountain, I turn down to the west and onto the main road.

'Hi, how ya going?' says a boy with red hair and a red T-shirt as he cycles past with a hurley under his arm. I beam back a greeting, and then notice him turning back to look at me as he pedals up the hill, obviously surprised by this apparition of a woman in a broad-brimmed hat.

About half a mile further, the Way turns off the main road again. It is late afternoon and a delicate gold light spreads across the land. A woman greets me from the doorway of her house as she looks out. A farmer moving some cows hails me. I stride along feeling utterly at one with the world again, until I have to scamper back when I discover I have dropped the map.

It is still about 9 miles to Ardmore, so I resist the temptation to deviate off the beaten track at the townland of Cross to look at some souterrains, underground tunnels which were apparently used for cold storage. The narrow country road runs along the crest of a hill and to the west I can see in the distance the wide Blackwater glistening silver in the sunlight as it makes its way down to the sea.

Now my mind is constantly calculating the miles I still have to go. Deep red fuchsias grow beside a white cottage with blue windows. A dead crow and a magpie hang from a farm gate, and dogs bark from driveways and gardens as I walk past.

Beyond the townland of Ballycurrane and down the hill I come to a T-junction, and there in front of me is a black wooden post and on it a white figure of a bishop holding a crozier—St Declan himself. A thick white arrow points to the path straight ahead. It is overgrown with nettles and brambles so I pick up a stick and hack my way through the undergrowth until it clears and opens out into a beech wood.

I walk under the beeches' green canopy down to the River Lickey, and in front of me are the stepping stones across what was known as the Ford of the Midges. Apparently, it was here that one of St Patrick's followers, a man called Ballin, drowned when travelling to Ardmore on an important mission to Declan. Declan was very upset when he heard what had happened and came immediately in his chariot from Ardmore to this spot, where he dropped to his knees in prayer, and Ballin was restored to life again.

I take off my shoes and socks and hop across the first couple of stepping stones to the middle of the river. I look for the one which is said to have Declan's foot imprinted in it, but can't make it out. With all the rain the river is in flood and flowing fast and the brown water is gushing over the top of the stepping stones in the middle. It's not a big, wide river like the Blackwater, but considering the fast current and the amount of water in it at the moment, I'm frightened of losing my footing on the stepping stones which are underwater and not sure whether it is too deep to wade across. Given Ballin's fate and the fact that no one would even be aware on this September evening that I was drowning in the Lickey—plus the note on the map, which says 'CAUTION! If Lickey River is flooded, do not attempt to use stepping stones. Detour via alternative route'—I err on the side of caution and reluctantly decide to turn back and take the longer way around via a bridge.

With still about 7 miles to Ardmore my mind is now rattling with calculations as to how fast I can walk in an hour, how much daylight I have, and deliberations as to whether I'll be able to find my way in the dark.

Back at the top of the path I turn left on to the road, which takes me downhill and westwards. Another road which forks off this one will take me across the river. I walk and walk, passing a forestry track, but there is no turning, and the sun is going down when eventually I reach some houses.

An elderly man is working in his shed and when I ask him where I am, I discover the main road is only a little further on, and the town of Clashmore about a mile along it. Better still, after my predicament in Aglish yesterday, I know there is a bed and breakfast there, so I head towards Clashmore, greatly relieved to be stopping for the night. Having worried how I was going to get to Ardmore before dark, I have been presented with the answer to my prayers.

The bed and breakfast is a modern house on the right just before the main street. When I ring the bell, a grey-haired man comes to the door. I ask for a room for the night but he tells me they are full and starts to close the door.

'I can't walk any further,' I wail, and explain that I'm following St Declan's Way. Then hastily add I have a sleeping bag and can sleep on the floor, but just need somewhere to stay. He tells me to hold on, leaves me standing on the doorstep and goes back into the house. A few minutes later he reappears, introduces himself as Noel, and shows me up a narrow staircase into a room with a double bed and a small ensuite bathroom, explaining that his wife, Teresa, had not wanted to have people staying this evening, but, of course, was happy to accommodate a pilgrim like me.

Relieved to dump my broken backpack I head out immediately to get something to eat, and find a small pub on the main street called the Decies Bar, with a painted sign of a man with a hurley. The girl behind the bar tells me food is only served on Friday and Saturday nights, which is no help given this is a Thursday. The only shop in town is the supermarket, which is where the woman in Villierstown this morning bought the mouldy apple pie, so with some reluctance I buy a cheese and salad roll and return to the pub where the girl gives me a large white plate to eat it on. I order a glass of Guinness and sink into a lounge chair.

I overhear one of the men at the bar explaining why Waterford didn't win the match. The last time the Déise reached the All-Ireland hurling final, he says, taking a sip of his pint, a group of supporters were heading to the match when a woman with a very sick child stopped them, and asked them to take the child and her to the hospital. The supporters told her they were already late for the match and drove off. The child died and it is said that the woman put a curse on the Déise, declaring they would not win an All-Ireland final for at least 50 years.

My feet hurt after the day's walking, so I hobble slowly down the main street under the light of the half moon and past the roadside shrine to Our Lady of the Wayside. There, in a sky blue alcove, is a statue of the Virgin Mary, her blue sash waving in the wind, her hands clasped together in prayer and a set of large rosary beads hanging off her arm. Her face is distinguished by two particularly blue eyes and bright red lips, and around her head is an impressive halo of electric lights.

I can't get the front door of the bed and breakfast open. After I fumble with my key for about five minutes, Noel appears and lets me in. I head straight to my room and fall completely exhausted into bed. I feel at a complete low point, as I am still 6 miles from Ardmore and don't even know how to get there.

The fairy fort and the high road

I wake at seven and, although my feet still hurt, with the new day I no longer feel overwhelmed. Downstairs, in the kitchen, Teresa is beside herself with excitement that I'm walking St Declan's Way, and says that in the eight years Noel and she have run the bed and breakfast they have never had a St Declan's Way walker staying with them.

Having told me to sit down at the table Teresa brings over a pot of tea and says she's going to tell her walking group all about me. She also tells me that she has been to the pattern at St Declan's Well of Toor, and that there were seven or eight priests present and coach loads of people.

Then she places a large plate in front of me, on which is bacon, sausages, black and white pudding, tomato and an egg. It is absolutely delicious and I suddenly realise how hungry I am. I eat everything plus several pieces of toast and marmalade and drink copious cups of tea. Out of the window

I can see a high brick tower built above the River Lickey which runs beside the garden. Teresa explains that the tower is all that remains of the Clashmore whiskey distillery, which in its five-year existence nearly 200 years ago produced 20 000 gallons of the spirit.

For once I am determined not to loiter, so immediately after breakfast I collect my backpack and leave.

'I hope you get enlightenment,' are Noel's parting words as he waves me on my way.

Walking back along the road to find the alternative river crossing, I stop briefly to admire some ox-eyed daisies growing along the verge. A man wearing a brown cap, green gumboots and a big green waterproof jacket, standing on the opposite side of the road, calls out, 'You're doing a lot of walking'.

When I explain that I'm on my way to Ardmore, he asks, 'Are you doing the mass path?' I assume I am unless another saint has been galavanting around here. He tells me the way to go.

The man's name is Lawrence Curran and he says he has land up the hill, adding that there are lots of Currans round here. I wonder if he is from the townland of Ballycurrane which I walked through yesterday evening. I assume he is about to move some sheep or cattle but he tells me he has come down to look at the new tarmac which has just been laid on the main road. 'We're getting very modern,' he muses, gazing at the fresh black bitumen.

Having turned off the main road I stop again to get directions from the same old man I asked last night. I notice in the clear light of day he is wearing on his head a wig of short brown hair, underneath which are the white wisps of his own hair. It looks like a toupee, but has been put on in such a haphazard way, with the thick black elastic showing, that I wonder if it is actually a hat.

He confirms the forestry track I passed last night does lead down to a bridge across the Lickey. Then he offers me a cup of tea, saying that if I'm walking I'll need it. Although I've already had four cups this morning, I'm very tempted to sit down and drink more tea with this man, if only to solve the mystery of the hat hair, but decide that today nothing must delay me getting to Ardmore.

After crossing the bridge and wandering along a path which soon turns into a stream, I start to seriously doubt my ability to read maps, as looking at the map again I realise I never should have veered onto this path in the first place. So I turn back to the bridge and set off again on what I hope is the right way. A pair of speckled wood butterflies circle above a briar of bright red rosehips, and I pass a blackthorn with its olive-shaped dark purple sloes.

Coming out onto a farm road I find a sign for St Declan's Way leaning upside-down against a wall. Much of the Way goes across farmers' land and I wonder if someone here has tired of pilgrims, perhaps because this last stretch is part of a thirteen and a half mile circuit walk from Ardmore.

Then, unbelievably, I see a rath in the field beside the road. Delighted I hop over a gate and walk towards it, at the same moment as a blue tractor comes up the road and also into the field. I run over to check the farmer doesn't mind me looking at the fairy fort on his land and he replies that it isn't a bother at all.

The rath is on a hill with long clear views in every direction. It is like a large bowl, about 20 to 25 yards in diameter, with earth sides on which hawthorn and gorse are growing. The farmer said it has not been touched, but on one side there is a gap in the bank and cattle obviously wander in and out of it. Given my propensity for losing my way, which fairies are known to cause, I have no intention of entering the rath, so instead I walk tentatively along the top of the earthen stone banks, wondering what fun and mischief might have been conjured up in the circle below me. Someone recently told me how he was taking a shortcut across a field one evening with a friend, and despite both of them knowing the field well, they were completely lost for quite a while, before they finally found their way out. Fairies are known for the temporary removal of gates and people recount stories of just having to sit and wait until they put them back again.

Exhilarated at having finally found a rath I continue on. Then back on the farm road I'm faced with a huge brown puddle, and no choice but to wade through it, and spend yet another day with soaking wet shoes and socks. Then the Way becomes a path again, with stone banks on either side of it, and fuchsia bushes dripping with their scarlet flowers. I pass a small gnarled apple tree with its trunk curling out from the bank and bearing apples half the size of cultivated ones. Looking at these small rosy round fruits, I'm immediately reminded of the choice they represent. It is as if this walk has shown me umpteen different options of how to be and to live, all attractive in their different ways, and now it is time to concentrate, choose one and enjoy its sweetness to the full, rather than taking an unsatisfactory bite from many.

I'm thinking hard about this—painfully aware of how torn I always am between wanting to taste and be a part of everything around me, and the desire to focus my attention on what is truly important—when I reach the bypass between Waterford and Cork and realise I am only a few miles from Ardmore.

Across the busy road I walk down the edge of a field, through a wooden kissing gate and onto a quiet back road. At the top of a hill is a school. I can only see a girl skipping beside the building, but hear a cacophony of children's voices and turn a corner to see them all out playing on the grass in their morning break. There is a game of football in progress, and another game which involves a ball and a variety of bats including tennis rackets and a blue plastic sword. A few children standing near the low stone wall say 'Hello' to me, and when I stop a host of others come rushing over. An older girl tells me this is Grange School and there are 80 pupils here, and immediately asks where I am from and why I am walking. As I'm talking to them, I suddenly get my first glimpse of the ocean in the distance.

'The sea,' I exclaim with excitement, to which one boy with very short hair tells me he has swam in it 26 times. When I enquire if it was cold, he replies, 'Freezing'. I ask if I can take their photograph with the sea behind them, and the children all cluster together and wave their hands in the air.

Leaving the school I make my way down to the bottom of the hill where an old well is marked on the map. There is a gate into the field where it is, but just as I'm about to climb over it, I notice a young black bull scraping the ground with his front hoof and snorting and throwing back his head like something out of a Greek myth. So I decide against that idea and continue walking up the next hill and onto a boreen known as *Bóthar Ard*, meaning 'high road'. It was to this road that emigrants from east of here were escorted by their family and friends, and their farewells said before they continued on to the ports of Youghal and Cobh to catch their boats to new worlds and new lives.

Elder and gorse are growing on the banks, and peeping through the clover and long grass is yellow tremanfoil and little blue speedwell. A white butterfly flutters over the hedgerow as I stop to pick blackberries and gaze at the brilliant aqua blue sea below, savouring the last moments of my journey along St Declan's Way.

At the bottom of this hill I'll be on the outskirts of Ardmore and soon my pilgrimage will be over. And in a few days time I'll be leaving Ireland once again and drawn back out into the world. Perhaps the only question I'm left with is, will I make good choices?

I reach the road to see a large white sign with 'Best of luck Clinton, Declan and Seamus' written in uneven blue letters, a message for the two Prenderghast brothers and Clinton Hennessy, the hurlers from Ardmore. Outside a terrace of houses blue and white flags are flying in the wind and there on the hill is the round tower. I have made it from Cashel to Ardmore.

It is said that on his return trip from Rome, Declan and his followers were crossing the Irish Sea when Runán, the son of the King of Rome, who came with Declan back to Ireland, realised that he had forgotten the miracle black bell which Declan had entrusted to him. Everyone prayed, and soon after saw a rock floating on the water with the bell on top. It passed the ship and Declan instructed the captain to follow it, saying that wherever it landed would be his city and bishopric, and the place of his resurrection. It came ashore here on a small island.

One of Declan's followers said, 'How can this little hill support your people?'

Declan replied, 'Do not call it a little hill but a great height' and that was how Ardmore got its name, because *Aird Mhór* in Irish means 'great height'. Declan went to the king of the Déisi and asked him for the island and the king gave it to him. But because the island was so small, Declan's followers implored him to either abandon the place or make the sea recede. So he struck the water with his crozier and prayed to God. The sea began to move out so quickly that the fish were left behind, and the island's shoreline increased by a mile in width.

40

You cannot draw blood from a turnip

Walking down the main street of Ardmore I see a bed and breakfast and decide to check in for the last night of my journey. Mary Maloney, who runs it, is showing me to my room, when I explain that I have walked from Cashel. Mary thinks this is wonderful and insists on introducing me to the other two guests that have just arrived, who look as if they are not particularly fond of walking, and have very little interest in anyone who is.

Then Mary tells me that, when St Declan's Way was first opened up again fifteen years ago, her son took the Ardmore scouts on the walk, starting in Cashel and camping along the way on the Knockmealdowns. She adds that the person who instigated the re-opening of St Declan's Way and organised the signposts along the route was Richard Lincoln. Richard is the man I rang about the map and who was in Africa, so his wife, Mary Lincoln, who runs Ardmore Pottery, sent me one instead. Richard's mother, Siobhan Lincoln, now in her 90s, rediscovered the Way and wrote a book about it, called *Along St Declan's Way*, which I now realise would have been a very helpful guide.

Mary also says that she attends every year on 23 July, the eve of St Declan's Day, the pattern by candlelight at Temple Dysert, the hermitage to which Declan used to retreat on the edge of the town.

The last section of the walk takes me past the Church of Ireland, which, of course, is firmly closed, to the ruined cathedral and round tower. It is here that Declan built a monastery 1600 years ago and it is believed to be the site of one of the oldest Christian settlements in Ireland.

On the hill is the perfectly preserved twelfth-century round tower, standing 97 feet tall, with its entrance door high off the ground and its conical cap roof like the one on the Rock of Cashel. Nearly four centuries ago it was besieged during the civil war when Irish Catholics rose in rebellion, hoping to recover the lands they had lost in the recent English plantations, and also concerned that the Puritan English Parliament might take away their freedom to practise Catholicism. Forty men with only two muskets installed themselves in the round tower, while their comrades defended the cathedral and Ardmore Castle, which no longer exists. But when Lord Broghill, the friend and follower of Oliver Cromwell, arrived with his artillery, they quickly surrendered. Broghill apparently showed little mercy and 117 out of 154 rebels were hanged.

There is a custom of walking around the tower three times clockwise and touching the stones of the tower while remembering this war and praying for peace and reconciliation between Protestants and Catholics. As I slowly run my fingers along over the grey stone, I think not just of this incident but of the other conflicts in the world.

The little building called the oratory, behind the ruined cathedral, originally contained the tomb of St Declan. The doorway is almost completely covered in earth, and the stone lintel is only a foot above the ground. I peer into the tiny dark stone building and hear the sound of cheeping, before a house martin flies out through the small window opening.

Within the walls of the ruined cathedral are two ogham stones. Ogham is an alphabet made up of lines, and Ireland's earliest writing. The stone on its side is engraved with five letters, AMADU, meaning 'The Loved One'. The letters of the ogham alphabet are named after trees and I am enthralled by the interconnectedness of nature and the written word. As I think about the letters they bring different parts of the walk into sharp focus. A is *Ailm*, the noble Scots pine I saw high up on the Round Hill between Lismore and Cappoquin. M is *Muin*, the bramble with which I have battled along the way. D is *Duir*, the Irish name for the mighty oak, the tree of the druids and St Brigid; and U is *Úr*, the beautiful purple heather which spreads itself across the Knockmealdowns.

I walk back through the churchyard and sit for a moment. In front of me on the west wall of the cathedral are two large stone arches, in which are motifs more than 1000 years old.

In the right arch is the story of the Judgment of Solomon. The stone carving shows King Solomon sitting on his throne holding a long sword, and in front of him one woman holding out the baby and behind her the second woman with outstretched arms, and then a mysterious figure of a harper sitting on a high stool. Underneath this in the stone arch is the nativity scene.

In the left arch of the wall is the story of temptation. This stone carving depicts the tree of knowledge, under which Eve is handing Adam the apple, and the serpent can be seen curling around the trunk and a low branch. Both Adam and Eve are also covering up their bodies with cloth.

How this scene differs from the great wisdom of Solomon and the birth of Jesus. Looking from one arch to the other, I realise that my life is a constant fluctuation between the two, from the moments of seeing the divine in everything, to feeling consumed by doubt and utterly isolated. I look up and there is a rainbow right across the sky.

With the final part of my pilgrimage to complete, I walk up the road beyond the round tower and follow the path along the cliffs to Father O'Donnell's Well. This stone structure was built over an ancient holy well, by a Mr Rahilly who came to Ardmore while recovering from an illness and found the well's water to have great curative properties. It was actually intended as a grotto for the Virgin Mary but was never finished, and instead stands as a timeless monument on the edge of the cliff.

I sit on the stone seat with the water flowing beneath it, and look out at the sea. Swallows swoop and dive around me. Below, waves gently roll up to the black rocks and break into a white foam, quietly roaring as they echo in the chasms they have worn away. I feel like a queen sitting here overlooking the world as I gaze down on a white gull that circles around a black rock peaking out of the water, and yet I also feel totally connected to everything around me.

I continue along the cliff path, lined with cushions of thrift and white-bladdered sea campion. A tortoiseshell butterfly flies ahead of me, and rests for a moment on a knapweed flower. A small white feather is cradled in the yellow gorse, and a young couple sit motionless on a bench looking out to sea. Then suddenly the stillness is broken by the squawking of black choughs and a mass of red bills and legs emerge as they whirl around on the sea breeze above the cliffs covered in bell heather.

The cliff path is a loop and I follow it towards the lower part of Ardmore. It was here, known as the Desert or Dísert, which means deserted place or heritage, Declan came for greater seclusion and built himself a little cell for solitude and prayer. Almost a mile away from the monastery, this was where he spent time in contemplation. Every year on the eve of St Declan's Day an all-night vigil is held here, and at midnight a mass is sometimes celebrated.

I sit on the stone step and listen to the water running into the cave-like stone building over the well. A rock dove drinks from the stream below it and flies up into a tree. I scoop the cool water into my hand and drink to my journey.

I didn't call myself a pilgrim when I set out from Cashel, and even halfway along St Declan's Way, when I was asked by the women staying at Glencairn whether I considered myself to be a pilgrim, I could not bring myself to say 'yes'. But now I realise I am.

My three-week journey has not only given me a far greater understanding of this land that I come from, but also made me look at my belief and faith. When I started this walk I thought my beliefs were more aligned with the Eastern philosophies of yoga and Buddhism than Christianity. To me Christianity was intolerant of other faiths, with totally unrealistic expectations of its followers in terms of belief. Also, I was disenfranchised by all the politics and power struggles which had gone on within the church. But now, at my destination, I can see that the core value of this faith is love. And to have that as a beacon is phenomenal. Love and the divine are one. I have seen it in the kindness of strangers and the generosity of friends, and in everything around me each day I have walked in sunshine or in rain along the ancient pathway.

Past the Cliff Hotel in the little harbour a couple of wooden painted boats are pulled up on the slipway, and just beyond here in the shallows I spot the infamous stone which floated ahead of St Declan's ship and brought him to Ardmore. The alternative opinion is that this piece of conglomerate rock broke away from the nearby Comeragh Mountains during the Ice Age more than 10 000 years ago and with the melting of the ice found its way here. It is poised like a mini dolmen on top of two rocks and it is said that crawling under it can bring healing. Once a priest who believed this practice was purely superstition brought a workman to break up the stone with a hammer. When they arrived at the stone, the workman said, 'You strike the first blow, Father, and I'll finish the job.' The priest declined.

My final port of call is St Declan's Catholic Church. Outside is a primitive painting of St Declan holding the cathedral and the round tower in his left hand. Inside on either side of the altar are statues of St Patrick and St Declan. These two men, so instrumental in the spread of Christianity in Ireland, are both wearing mitres and holding croziers and a book of the gospels. St Patrick is also holding a shamrock and is standing on a snake.

As a final gesture I want to light a candle, but can't find any matches in the church, so walk up the main street to buy some. At the shop the woman behind the counter sells me a small box of Cara safety matches, on the bottom of which is printed in Irish and beside it in English, 'You cannot draw blood from a turnip'.

I kneel in front of the three candles I have lit at the side altar at the feet of a statue of the Virgin Mary and ponder on whether this riddle is about knowing one's own limitations, being aware of other peoples', or knowing about turnips, then decide it probably has some other meaning I haven't even considered.

Finally, puffed up with pride like a pigeon, having completed my pilgrimage, I strut up to see Mary Lincoln at Ardmore Pottery, who sent me the map of the Way, bursting to tell her about my battles with brambles and slaying of stingers. I find her sitting at a wheel, busy making clay plaques for some pots. She tells me not to worry about paying her for the postage and adds that a few people are doing the walk each year. Then she apologises and says she can't stop to talk as the plaques need to be finished today. After expecting a hero's welcome after all my trials and tribulations, I thank her and turn tail.

I walk down onto the beach in front of the sea wall and gaze at the water lapping against the pebbles. Then I pick up a flat round stone, throw it into the sea and watch the ever-widening circle of ripples as it hits the surface of the water and sinks to the bottom.

Information for someone wanting to follow St Declan's Way

I have included the details of the places where I stayed and also the places I visited. I have listed hotels or bed and breakfasts in places where I stayed with friends. I have also listed the local tourist information centres for further details.

For a map of St Declan's Way, contact
Ardmore Pottery and Craft Shop
353 (0)24 94152
mary@ardmorepottery.com
www.ardmorepottery.com

Bus Eireann
For buses to Cashel and from Ardmore
353 (0)1 8366111

Cashel, County Tipperary

Cashel Heritage Centre and Tourist Information Centre
Main Street, Cashel
353 (0)62 62511
www.cashel.ie

O'Brien's Cashel Lodge
Rock House, Cashel
353 (0)62 61003
info@cashel-lodge.com
www.cashel-lodge.com

Daverns Pub
20 Main Street, Cashel
353 (0)62 61121

The Rock of Cashel
Open daily
353 (0)62 61437
rockofcashel@opw.ie

The Bolton Library
John Street, Cashel
Open Monday to Friday 10 a.m. to 4 p.m. Group tours by
appointment
353 (0)62 61944
boltonlibrary@oceanfree.net

Cahir, County Tipperary

Cahir Tourist Information Centre
Castle Car Park, Cahir
This is a seasonal office.
353 (0)52 7441453
cahir@failteireland.ie
www.discoverireland.ie/tipperary

Lisakyle Hostel
Open April to September.
The house opposite the post office in Church Street, Cahir,
handles inquiries and arranges lifts to the hostel.
353 (0)52 7441963

The Galtee Inn
The Square, Cahir
353 (0)52 7441247

The Lazy Bean Café
The Square, Cahir
353 (0)52 7442038

Swiss Cottage
Kilcommon, Cahir
Open daily from April to October. Admission by guided tour
only. Groups of 10 or more must be pre-booked.
353 (0)52 7441144
swisscottage@opw.ie

Cahir Castle
Castle Street, Cahir
Open daily
353 (0)52 7441011
cahircastle@opw.ie

Ardfinnan

I did not stay in Ardfinnan but at Castle Grace. Castle Grace has holiday lets and Kilmaneen Farmhouse near Ardfinnan does bed and breakfast. For more information about accommodation, contact Cahir Tourist Information Centre.

Castle Grace
353 (0)86 8186305
bgrubb@eircom.net
www.vee.ie

Kilmaneen Farmhouse
353 (0)52 6136231
info@kilmaneen.com
www.kilmaneen.com

The Knockmealdown Mountains and Mount Melleray, County Waterford

On the Knockmealdowns it is possible to stay at The Pilgrims Rest and also the guesthouse at Mount Melleray Abbey.

Mount Melleray Abbey
Mount Melleray, Cappoquin
353 (0)58 54404
guestmaster@mountmellerayabbey.org
www.mountmellerayabbey.org

The Pilgrims Rest Hotel
Mount Melleray, Cappoquin
353 (0)58 52971
www.thepilgrimsrest.com

The Cat's Bar
Boola, Cappoquin
353 (0)58 54150
thecatsbar@eircom.net

Mount Melleray Grotto
www.melleray.com

Lismore, County Waterford

Lismore House Hotel provides accommodation. For more information on accommodation and the area in general, contact the Lismore Heritage Centre and Tourist Information Centre.

Lismore Heritage Centre and Tourist Information Office
West Street, Lismore
353 (0)58 54975
lismoreheritage@eircom.net
www.discoverlismore.com

Lismore House Hotel
Main Street, Lismore
353 (0)58 72966
www.lismorehousehotel.com

Lismore Castle
Lismore
The Lismore Castle gardens are open daily from 17 March to 30 September.
353 (0)58 54424
gardens@lismorecastle.com
www.lismorecastle.com

St Mary's Abbey
Glencairn
353 (0)58 56168
info@glencairnabbey.org
www.glencairnabbey.org

Cappoquin, County Waterford

You can stay at the River View Guesthouse. For more information on accommodation in the Cappoquin area, contact the Lismore Heritage Centre and Tourist Information Centre.

River View Guesthouse
Cook Street, Cappoquin
353 (0)58 54073
riverviewguesthouse@hotmail.com

Tourin House and Gardens
Cappoquin
Open from April to September. Tuesday to Saturday, 1 p.m. to 5 p.m. Groups by appointment.
353 (0)58 54405
tourin@eircom.net

Cappoquin House and Gardens
Cappoquin
Open from April to July. Monday to Saturday, 9 a.m. to 1 p.m. Open all year for tours by appointment.
353 (0)58 54290 (mornings)
charleskeane@cappoquinestate.com

Dromana House and Gardens
Villierstown
Open from April to June, 2 p.m. to 6 p.m. Open all year round for tours by appointment. Self-catering apartments are also available.
353 (0)24 96144
bgrubb@eircom.net
www.dromanahouse.com

Clashmore, County Waterford

Riverside B&B
Clashmore
353 (0)24 96135
potstill@eircom.net

The Decies Bar
Clashmore
353 (0)24 96402

Ardmore, County Waterford

For more information on Ardmore, including accommodation, contact the Dungarvan Tourist Office.

Dungarvan Tourist Office
353 (0)58 41741
www.dungarvantourism.com

Fountain House B&B
Ardmore
353 (0)24 94256
fountainhouse@eircom.net

Ardmore Pottery and Craft Shop
The Cliff, Ardmore
353 (0)24 94152
mary@ardmorepottery.com
www.ardmorepottery.com

Helpful books

Blarney, Marjorie and Fitter, Richard (1980) *Wild Flowers*, Glasgow: Collins

Cahill, Thomas (1995) *How the Irish Saved Civilisation*, London: Hodder and Stoughton

Murray, Liz and Colin (1988) *The Celtic Tree Oracle: A System of Divination*, New York: St Martin's Press

Egan, Ann (2001) *Brigit of Kildare*, Kildare County Council Library and Arts Service

Fitter, Alastair and More, David (1980) *Trees*, Glasgow: HarperCollins Publishers

Foster, Robert Fitzroy (ed) (1992) *The Oxford History of Ireland*, Oxford University Press

Graham, Mark and Buchan, Heather (2006) *The Celtic Tree Ogham: Pathways Through the Inner Forest*, Somerset: Capall Bann Publishing

Graves, Alfred Perceval (2005) *The Irish Fairy Book*, New York: Dover Publications

Graves, Robert (1999) *The White Goddess*, London: Faber and Faber

Harpur, Patrick (1994) *Daimonic Reality: A Field Guide to the Other World*, London: Penguin Group

Jones, Kathy (2001) *The Ancient British Goddess*, Glastonbury, Somerset: Ariadne Publications

Kee, Robert (2006) *Ireland: A History*, London: Abacus

Kelly, Sister Veronica Gertrude (2005) *Glimpses of Glencairn*, Glencairn, Co Waterford: St Mary's Abbey

Lincoln, Siobhan (2004) *Along St Declan's Way*, self-published

Mac Coitr, Niall (2003) *Irish Trees: Myths, Legends & Folklore*, Cork: The Collins Press

Mac Coitr, Niall (2008) *Irish Wild Plants: Myths, Legends & Folklore*, Cork: The Collins Press

MacKenzie, Thérèse Muir (1906) *Dromana: The Memoirs of an Irish Family*, Dublin: Sealy, Bryers and Walker

McCarthy, Thomas (1998) *Gardens of Remembrance*, Dublin: New Island Books

McKinney, Donald (2005) *Celtic Angels*, London: Hodder and Stoughton

McMahon, Joanne and Roberts, Jack (2000) *The Sheela-Na-Gigs of Ireland and Britain*, Dublin: Mercier Press

Minehan, Rita (1999) *Rekindling the Flame*, Kildare: Solas Bhríde Community

Newby, Eric (1988) *Round Ireland in Low Gear*, London: Pan Books Ltd

Ó Duinn, Seán (2000) *Where Three Streams Meet: Celtic Spirituality*, Dublin: The Columba Press

O'Sullivan, Melanie and McCarthy, Kevin (1999) *Cappoquin: A Walk Through History*

Pennick, Nigel (1996) *Celtic Sacred Landscapes*, New York: Thames & Hudson

Power, Reverend P (1914) Edited from MS in Bibliotheque Royale, Brussels. Translated from the Irish with introduction, *Life of St Declan of Ardmore*

Power, Reverend P (1903) 'The "Rian Bó Phádraig" The Ancient Highway of the Decies': paper presented to the Royal Society of Antiquities of Ireland

Toibín, Colm (ed.) (1985) *Seeing is Believing: Moving Statues in Ireland*, Mountrath, Co Laois: Pilgrim Press

White, Caroline (2001), *A History of Irish Fairies*, Mercier Press, Dublin